Top Student Workbook
Grade 1

This book belongs to:

Editorial Development: Teera Safi
Kathleen Jorgensen
Lisa Vitarisi Mathews
Vicky Shiotsu
Copy Editing: Cathy Harber
Art Direction: Yuki Meyer
Cover Design: Yuki Meyer
Illustration: Mary Rojas
Chris Vallo
Design: Jessica Onken
Production: Susan Lovell

EMC 9321

Evan-Moor
Helping Children Learn

Visit
teaching-standards.com
to view a correlation
of this book.
This is a free service.

**Correlated to
Current Standards**

**Congratulations on your purchase of some of the
finest teaching materials in the world.**

EVAN-MOOR CORP.
phone 1-800-777-4362, fax 1-800-777-4332.
Entire contents © 2020 EVAN-MOOR CORP.
18 Lower Ragsdale Drive, Monterey, CA 93940-5746. Printed in USA.

CPSIA: Hess Print Solutions, Brimfield, OH USA [1/2020]

Contents

What's Inside

Top Student Workbook provides practice in core subject areas as well as opportunities for critical thinking and creativity across the curriculum!

Children are learning new concepts and skills throughout the year. The activities in this book practice the most important grade-level skills and provide a path for academic success, building children's confidence as well as social-emotional and communication skills.

We've included Mindful Moments with audio so children will learn to incorporate reflection and meditation into their academic lives. We've also included social and emotional learning (SEL) activities across the curriculum. These kinds of activities provide an opportunity for children to work on self-awareness, personal responsibility, empathy, optimistic thinking, and decision making, among other skills.

Children will also encounter information and activities about a variety of countries, cultures, and global communities.

We are honored to provide activities and practice that will lead to children's academic success, and we celebrate your child for being a Top Student!

Handwriting

Write A, B, and C

Copy the letters.

ant

bat

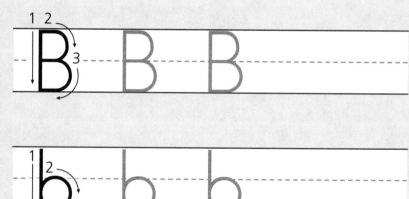

cat

Write D, E, and F

Copy the letters.

dog

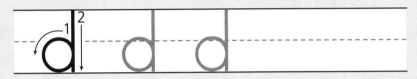

elephant

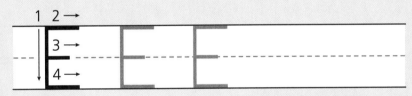

fox

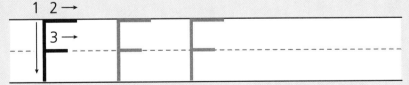

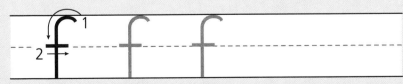

Write G, H, and I

Copy the letters.

goat

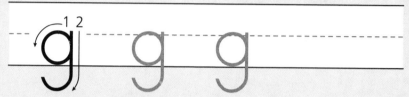

hamster

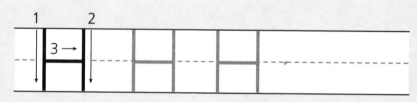

iguana

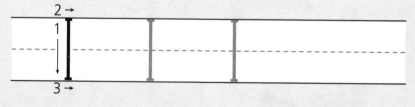

Top Student • EMC 9321 • © Evan-Moor Corp.

Write J, K, and L

Copy the letters.

jellyfish

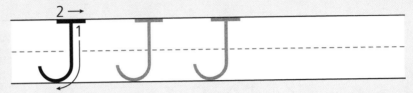

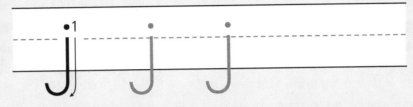

koala

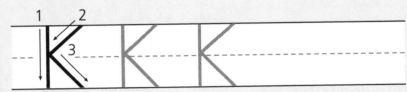

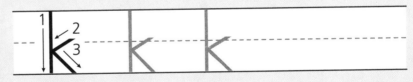

lion

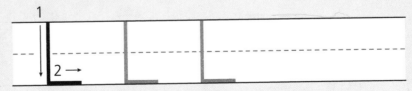

Write M, N, and O

Copy the letters.

mouse

nest

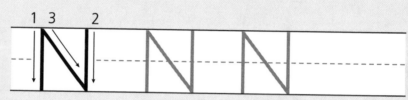

octopus

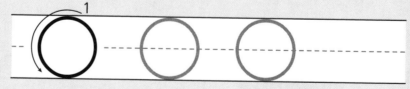

Write P, Q, and R

Copy the letters.

penguin

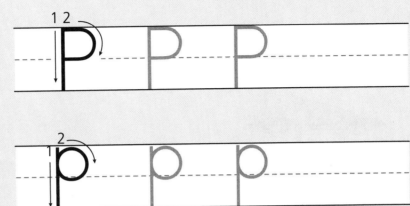

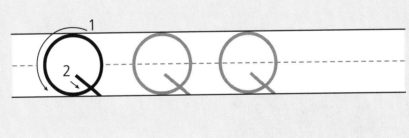

quail

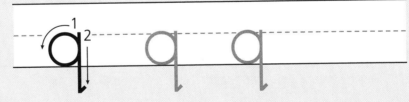

rabbit

Write S, T, and U

Copy the letters.

seal

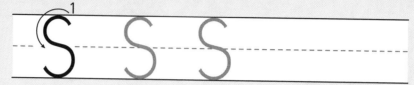

tiger

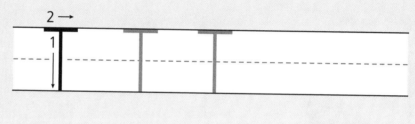

unicorn

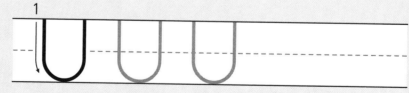

Top Student • EMC 9321 • © Evan-Moor Corp.

Write V, W, and X

Copy the letters.

vulture

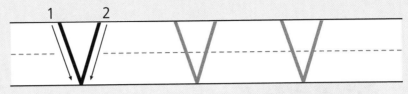

walrus

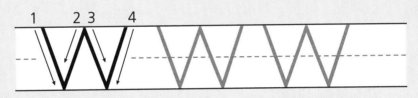

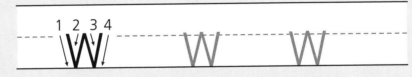

ox

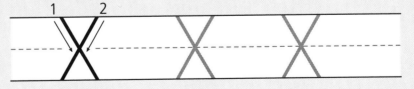

Write Y and Z

Copy the letters.

yak

zebra

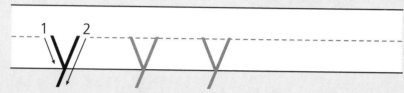

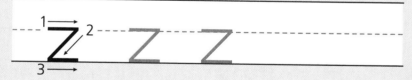

Write Words from a List

Look at Lucy's list. Then look at the picture of foods Lucy has on the table. Write the name of each food on the list below that Lucy does not have yet.

List

- apple
- carrots
- milk
- chocolate bar
- green beans
- cereal
- chips
- pretzels
- lemonade
- ice cream

Lucy still needs:

_____   _____

_____   _____

_____   _____

_____   _____

What I Like!

SKILLS
Social and Emotional Learning: Demonstrate a positive self-image; Reflect on positive attributes of others

Read the items. Use your best handwriting to write sentences.

This is what I like about...

1. Write to tell one thing you like about **yourself**.

   _____

   _____

2. Write to tell one thing you like about **your best friend**.

   _____

   _____

3. Write to tell one thing you like about **your family**.

   _____

   _____

4. Write to tell one thing you like about **animals**.

   _____

   _____

Phonics

Consonants at the Beginning of Words

Say the picture name. Then write the letter that stands for the **first** sound you hear.

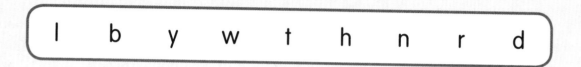

l   b   y   w   t   h   n   r   d

1.

_____all

2.

_____amp

3.

_____eb

4.
10
_____en

5.

_____og

6.

_____at

7.

_____est

8.

_____and

9.

_____arn

Write the Beginning Consonant

Say the picture name. Then write the letter that stands for the **first** sound you hear.

| z | s | p | v | m | j | k | f | b |

1.
____an

2.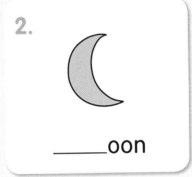
____oon

3.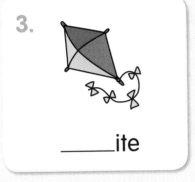
____ite

4.
____ie

5.
____ock

6.
____an

7.
____ar

8.
____ox

9.
____ebra

Hard and Soft C

Sometimes the letter **c** has the first sound you hear in **cup**. This is called the **hard c** sound.

cup

Sometimes the letter **c** has the first sound you hear in **celery**. This is called the **soft c** sound.

celery

Say the picture name. Read the word.
Then circle the word if you hear a **soft c**.

1.
cent

2.
coat

3.
cave

4.
corn

5.
circle

6.
city

Top Student • EMC 9321 • © Evan-Moor Corp.

Hard and Soft G

Sometimes the letter **g** has the first sound you hear in **gate**. This is called the **hard g** sound.

gate

Sometimes the letter **g** has the first sound you hear in **gem**. This is called the **soft g** sound.

gem

Say the picture name. Read the word.
Then circle the word if you hear a **soft g**.

1.

gum

2.

gem

3.

girl

4.

giant

5.

gift

6.

goat

Say the picture name. Then write the letter that stands for the **last** sound you hear.

d   n   g   t   m   b

1.

gu_____

2.

ba_____

3.
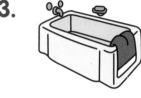
tu_____

4.

fla_____

5.

fa_____

6.

be_____

7.

je_____

8.

ba_____

9.

su_____

Write the End Consonant

Say the picture name. Then write the letter that stands for the **last** sound you hear.

l   s   p   f   r   k

1.

bu_____

2.

mo_____

3.

boo_____

4.

snai_____

5.

ja_____

6.

lea_____

7.

ma_____

8.

for_____

9.

ow_____

The Letters Q and X

The letter **q** has the first sound you hear in **quilt**.

quilt

Sometimes the letter **x** has the last sound you hear in **mix**.

mi**x**

Look at the picture. Then write a **q** or an **x** to finish the word.

1.

_____ueen

2.

fo_____

3.

_____uail

The Letters -s and -es

We add an **-s** or **-es** to the end of some nouns to make them plural.

Sometimes **s** has the last sound you hear in **cakes**. This is an **s sound**.

cake**s**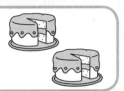

Sometimes **s** has the last sound you hear in **apples**. This is a **z sound**.

apple**s**

Look at the pictures. Read the word.
Then fill in the circle by the sound you hear at the **end**.

1. cats

○ **s** sound
○ **z** sound

2. webs

○ **s** sound
○ **z** sound

3. bikes

○ **s** sound
○ **z** sound

4. cakes

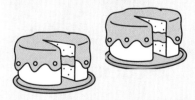

○ **s** sound
○ **z** sound

5. foxes

○ **s** sound
○ **z** sound

6. nets

○ **s** sound
○ **z** sound

Syllables

A **syllable** is a word part that has one vowel sound.

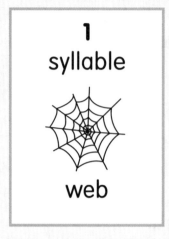

1
syllable

web

2
syllables

wagon

Say the picture name. How many vowel sounds do you hear?
Fill in the circle next to the correct number.

1. hippo
   ○ 1
   ○ 2

2. bone
   ○ 1
   ○ 2

3. baby
   ○ 1
   ○ 2

4. hen
   ○ 1
   ○ 2

5. monkey
   ○ 1
   ○ 2

6. cactus
   ○ 1
   ○ 2

The letter **a** is a vowel. Sometimes it has the middle sound you hear in **hat**. This is called the **short a** sound.

| short **a** | | hat |

Say the picture name. Fill in the circle next to **yes** if you hear the sound of **short a**. Fill in the circle next to **no** if you do <u>not</u> hear the sound of **short a**.

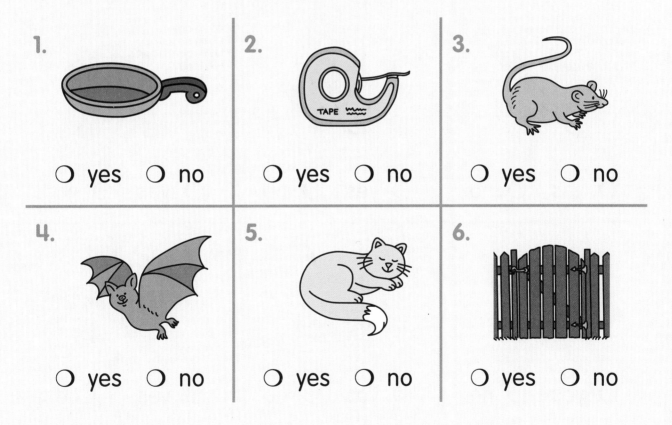

1. ○ yes ○ no

2. ○ yes ○ no

3. ○ yes ○ no

4. ○ yes ○ no

5. ○ yes ○ no

6. ○ yes ○ no

Fill in **yes** or **no** to answer the question.

7. Does your name have the **short a** sound?   ○ yes   ○ no

Short Vowel E

The letter **e** is a vowel. Sometimes it has the middle sound you hear in **ten**. This is called the **short e** sound.

| short e | 10 | ten |

Say the picture name. Fill in the circle next to **yes** if you hear the sound of **short e**. Fill in the circle next to **no** if you do <u>not</u> hear the sound of **short e**.

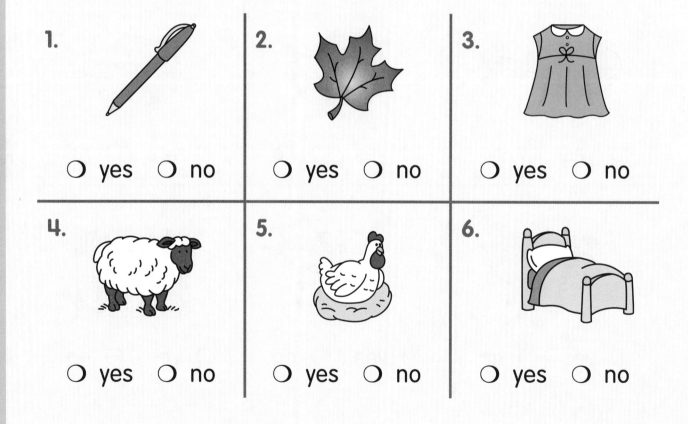

1. ○ yes   ○ no
2. ○ yes   ○ no
3. ○ yes   ○ no
4. ○ yes   ○ no
5. ○ yes   ○ no
6. ○ yes   ○ no

Fill in **yes** or **no** to answer the question.

7. Does your name have the **short e** sound?   ○ yes   ○ no

Short Vowel I

The letter **i** is a vowel. Sometimes it has the middle sound you hear in **sit**. This is called the **short i** sound.

short **i**		sit

Say the picture name. Fill in the circle next to **yes** if you hear the sound of **short i**. Fill in the circle next to **no** if you do <u>not</u> hear the sound of **short i**.

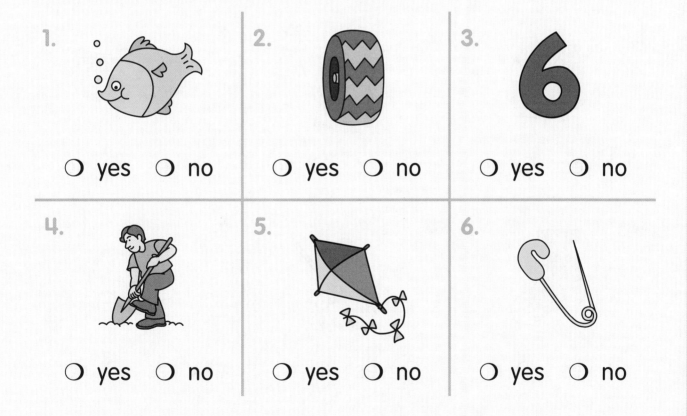

1. ○ yes ○ no

2. ○ yes ○ no

3. ○ yes ○ no

4. ○ yes ○ no

5. ○ yes ○ no

6. ○ yes ○ no

Fill in **yes** or **no** to answer the question.

7. Does your name have the **short i** sound?   ○ yes ○ no

Short Vowel O

The letter **o** is a vowel. Sometimes it has the middle sound you hear in **fox**. This is called the **short o** sound.

| short **o** | | fox |

Say the picture name. Fill in the circle next to **yes** if you hear the sound of **short o**. Fill in the circle next to **no** if you do <u>not</u> hear the sound of **short o**.

1. ○ yes ○ no

2. ○ yes ○ no

3. ○ yes ○ no

4. ○ yes ○ no

5. ○ yes ○ no

6. ○ yes ○ no

Fill in **yes** or **no** to answer the question.

7. Does your name have the **short o** sound?   ○ yes ○ no

Short Vowel U

The letter **u** is a vowel. Sometimes it has the middle sound you hear in **bug**. This is called the **short u** sound.

| short **u** | | b**u**g |

Say the picture name. Fill in the circle next to **yes** if you hear the sound of **short u**. Fill in the circle next to **no** if you do <u>not</u> hear the sound of **short u**.

1. ○ yes ○ no

2. ○ yes ○ no

3. ○ yes ○ no

4. ○ yes ○ no

5. ○ yes ○ no

6. ○ yes ○ no

Fill in **yes** or **no** to answer the question.

7. Does your name have the **short u** sound? ○ yes ○ no

Long Vowel Sounds
of A and I

The vowels **a** and **i** have **long** sounds.
The **long a** and **long i** sounds say the vowels' names.

long **a** c**a**ke	

long **i** b**i**ke	

a   i

Say the picture name. Then write the letter that stands for
the **long** vowel sound you hear.

1. k___te	2. 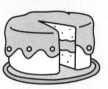 c___ke	3. n___ne
4.  g___te	5.  t___pe	6.  b___ke
7.  r___ke	8. d___me	9.  c___ge

Long Vowel Sounds of E and O

The vowels **e** and **o** have **long** sounds.
The **long e** and **long o** sounds say the vowels' names.

long **e** h**e**		long **o** b**o**ne	

Say the picture name. Then write the letter that stands for the **long** vowel sound you hear.

1.  w____	2. r____be	3.  b____ne
4.  n____se	5.  h____	6. r____pe
7.  sh____	8.  c____ne	9.  m____

Long Vowel Sounds of U

The vowel **u** has a **long** sound.

Sometimes the **long u** sound says the vowel's name.	long **u** m**u**le

Sometimes the **long u** sound has the vowel sound you hear in **blue**.	long **u** bl**ue** 

Look at the picture. Read the word.
What kind of **long u** sound does the word have?
Fill in the circle by the word that has the same sound.

1. cube
   - ○ mule
   - ○ blue

2. flute
   - ○ mule
   - ○ blue

3. tune
   - ○ mule
   - ○ blue

4. huge
   - ○ mule
   - ○ blue

5. glue
   - ○ mule
   - ○ blue

6. cute
   - ○ mule
   - ○ blue

CVC Words

A **CVC word** is a word that has a vowel between 2 consonants. The word has 3 letters. The vowel in a CVC word has a **short** vowel sound.

cat

mug

Say the picture name. Read the words.
Then fill in the circle next to the word that names the picture.

1.
○ tub
○ tab

2.
○ map
○ mop

3.
○ jut
○ jet

4.
○ bat
○ bet

5.
○ rag
○ rug

6.
○ fix
○ fox

7.
○ bad
○ bed

8.
○ cup
○ cap

9.
○ dog
○ dig

CVCe Words

When an **e** is added to a CVC word, it makes the vowel sound **long**. The **e** is silent, but it changes the vowel sound in the middle of the word.

 man + **e** = mane

Write an **e** to make the vowel sound **long**.
Then read the word. Fill in the circle under the picture that matches the new word you made.

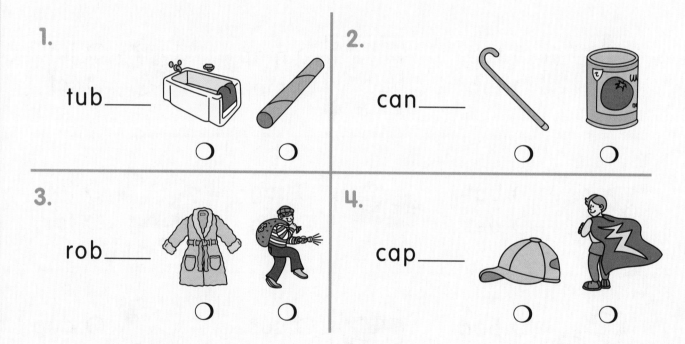

1.

tub____

○   ○

2.

can____

○   ○

3.

rob____

○   ○

4.

cap____

○   ○

Write one more word that has a **silent e** at the end.

5. _____

Sometimes the letter **y** has the **long i** or the **long e** sound.

	**y = long i** fl**y**			**y = long e** bab**y**

Say the word. What sound does the **y** stand for?
Fill in the circle next to the **long i** or the **long e**.

1.
○ long i
○ long e
cr**y**

2.
○ long i
○ long e
pupp**y**

3.
○ long i
○ long e
happ**y**

4.
○ long i
○ long e
fr**y**

5.
○ long i
○ long e
bunn**y**

6.
○ long i
○ long e
sk**y**

Write one more word that has the **long i** sound and ends in **y**.

7. _____

Long A Sound Digraphs

A **digraph** is two letters together that stand for a sound.

The digraphs **ai** and **ay** can stand for the **long a** sound.

| p**ai**l | 🪣 | | j**ay** | 🐦 |

Say the picture name. Read the word.
Then underline the letters that stand for the **long a** sound.

1. clay

2. rain

3. snail

4. train

5. spray

6. mail

Write one more word that has the **long a** sound.

7. _____

Top Student • EMC 9321 • © Evan-Moor Corp.

A **digraph** is two letters together that stand for a sound.

The digraphs **ee** and **ea** can stand for the **long e** sound.

b**ee**   l**ea**f

Say the picture name. Read the word.
Then underline the letters that stand for the **long e** sound.

1. peach

2. cheese

3. sleep

4. teeth

5. seal

6. feet

Write one more word that has the **long e** sound.

7. _____

The **long i** sound can be spelled **ie** or **igh**.

| p**ie** | | l**igh**t | |

Say the picture name. Read the word.
Then underline the letters that stand for the **long i** sound.

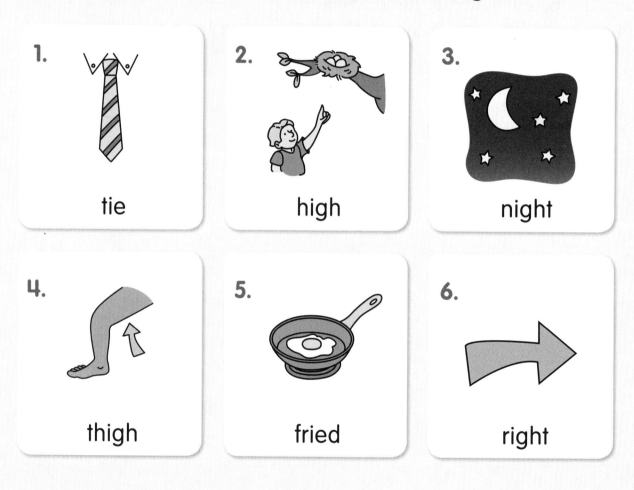

1. tie

2. high

3. night

4. thigh

5. fried

6. right

Write one more word that has the **long i** sound.

7. _____

Long O Sound Digraphs

A **digraph** is two letters together that stand for a sound.

The digraphs **oe**, **ow**, and **oa** can stand for the **long o** sound.

Say the picture name. Read the word.
Then underline the letters that stand for the **long o** sound.

1. toe

2. toast

3. snow

4. soap

5. bow

6. boat

Write one more word that has the **long o** sound.

7. _____

Letter Pairs: oi and oy

The letter pairs **oi** and **oy** can stand for the middle sounds you hear in **coin** and **boy**.

coin		boy	

Say the picture name. Read the word.
Then underline the letters that stand for
the vowel sound you hear in **coin** and **boy**.

1. toy

2. soil

3. joy

4. boil

5. point

6. oil

Letter Pairs: **ow** and **ou**

Some letter pairs stand for certain sounds.
The letter pairs **ow** and **ou** can stand for the
vowel sound you hear in **cow** and **mouse**.

Say the picture name. Read the word.
Then underline the letters that stand for
the vowel sound you hear in **cow** and **mouse**.

1. 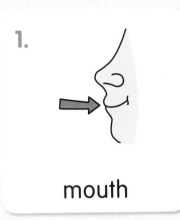	2. 	3. 
mouth	house	clown

4. 	5. 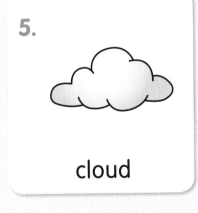	6. 
owl	cloud	crown

Letter Pair: oo

Some letter pairs have certain sounds. The letter pair **oo** can stand for the middle sound you hear in **moon**. It can also stand for the middle sound you hear in **book**.

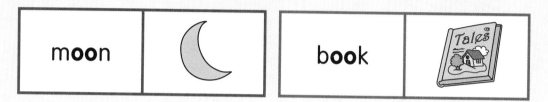

Name the first picture. Listen to the vowel sound. Then name each picture in the row. Fill in the circle if it has the **same** vowel sound as the first picture.

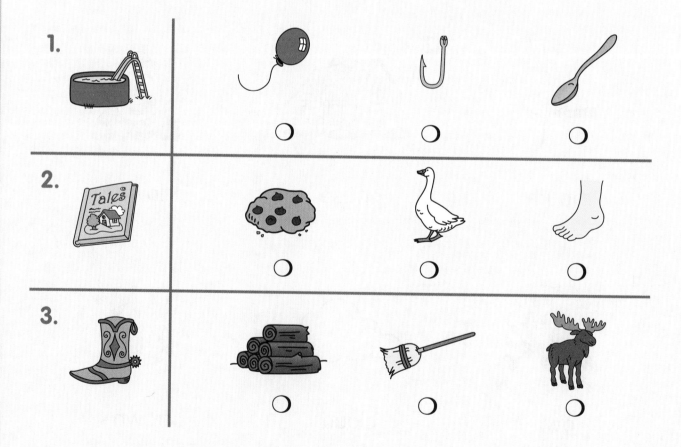

Initial Consonant Blends

Two consonant sounds said together are called
a **consonant blend**. These are consonant blends.

Say the sound of the blend. Then say each picture name.
Fill in the circle if the picture name **begins** with that blend.

Write Initial Consonant Blends

Many words begin with a **consonant blend**.
These are consonant blends.

sk		sm		sp	

Say the sounds of the blends in the box below.
Then say the picture name. Listen to the letter-sounds.
Last, write the blend to finish the word.

sk   sm   sp

1. _____ _____oon

2. _____ _____ell

3. _____ _____unk

4. _____ _____y

5. _____ _____ate

6. _____ _____ider

7. _____ _____irt

8. _____ _____oke

9. _____ _____y

Blends with the Letter L

Many words begin with a **consonant blend**.
These are consonant blends.

Say the sound of the blend. Then say each picture name.
Fill in the circle if the picture name **begins** with that blend.

1. fl-

2. cl-

3. sl-

More Blends with L

Many words begin with a **consonant blend**.
These are consonant blends.

pl		bl		gl	

Say the sounds of the blends in the box below.
Then say the picture name. Listen to the letter-sounds.
Last, write the blend to finish the word.

> pl   bl   gl

1.	2.	3.
____ ____ove	____ ____ant	____ ____ow
4.	5.	6.
____ ____ane	____ ____ock	____ ____obe
7.	8.	9.
____ ____ack	____ ____ue	____ ____ass

Top Student • EMC 9321 • © Evan-Moor Corp.

Many words begin with a **consonant blend**.
These are consonant blends.

Say the sound of the blend. Then say each picture name.
Fill in the circle if the picture name **begins** with that blend.

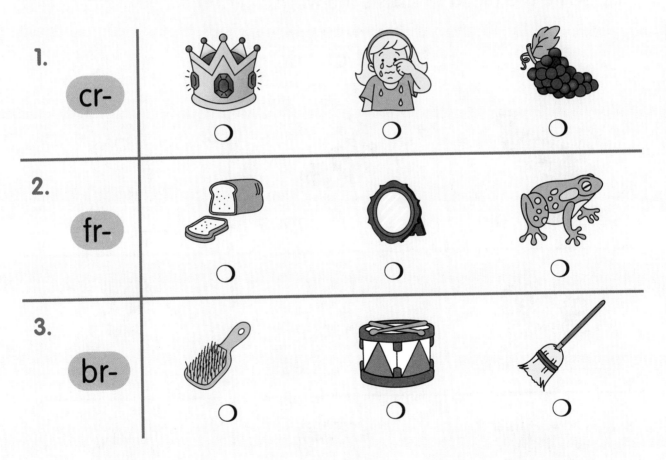

1. cr-

2. fr-

3. br-

More Blends with R

Many words begin with a **consonant blend**.
These are consonant blends.

 tr gr dr

Say the sounds of the blends in the box below.
Then say the picture name. Listen to the letter-sounds.
Last, write the blend to finish the word.

> tr   gr   dr

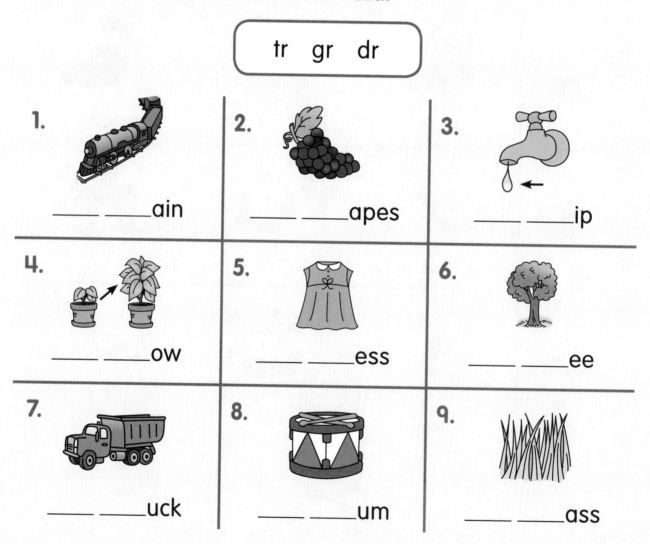

1. _____ _____ain

2. _____ _____apes

3. _____ _____ip

4. _____ _____ow

5. _____ _____ess

6. _____ _____ee

7. _____ _____uck

8. _____ _____um

9. _____ _____ass

Final Consonant Blends

Many words end with a **consonant blend**.
These are consonant blends.

 st    lt    nk

Say the sound of the blend. Then say each picture name.
Fill in the circle if the picture name **ends** with that blend.

1. -st

2. -lt

3. -nk

Write Final Consonant Blends

Many words end with a **consonant blend**.
These are consonant blends.

lf		**nt**		**mp**	

Say the sounds of the blends in the box below.
Then say the picture name. Listen to the letter-sounds.
Last, write the blend to finish the word.

| lf   nt   mp |

1. wo_____ _____

2. la_____ _____

3. she_____ _____

4. a_____ _____

5. e_____ _____

6. te_____ _____

7. pla_____ _____

8. ju_____ _____

9. sta_____ _____

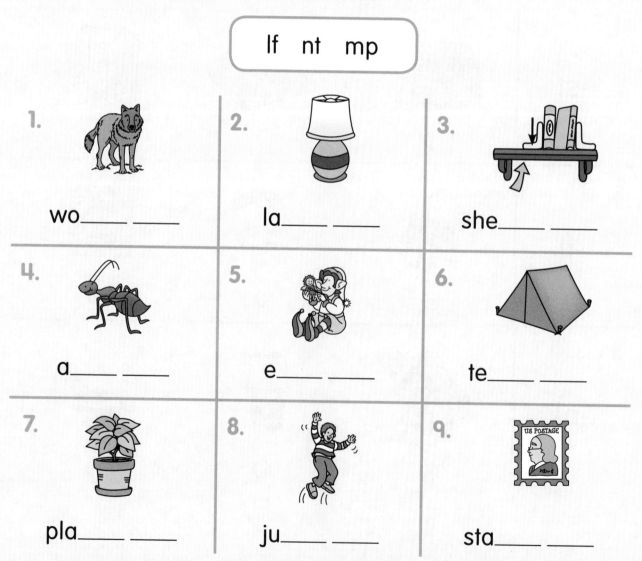

Consonant Blends in Words

Words can begin or end with a **consonant blend**.

stop		ne**st**	

Say the sound of the blend. Then say the picture name.
Fill in the circle to show if you hear the blend **first** or **last**.

1. cl

○——○

2. mp

○——○

3. tr

○——○

4. lt
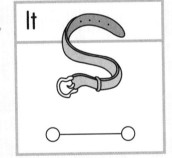
○——○

5. st

○——○

6. br

○——○

7. lf

○——○

8. sp
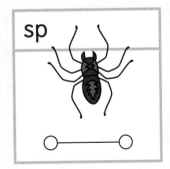
○——○

9. sk

○——○

Initial Consonant Digraphs

Sometimes two letters together have one sound.

| sh | 🐑 | th | 3 | wh | 🐋 |

Say the sound of the two letters. Then say each picture name.
Fill in the circle if the picture name **begins** with that sound.

1. sh-

2. th-

3. wh-

Final Consonant Digraphs

Many words end with the digraphs **sh**, **ch**, or **th**.

| **sh** | | **ch** | | **th** | |

Say the sound of the two letters. Then say each picture name.
Fill in the circle if the picture name **ends** with that sound.

1. **-sh**

○   ○   ○

2. **-ch**

○   ○   ○

3. **-th**

○   ○   ○

Fill Your Cup

SKILLS
Analyze words; Social and Emotional
Learning: Demonstrates self-awareness

Pretend that when you feel happy, your cup is full. When you feel unhappy, your cup is empty. Now it's time to fill your cup. On each line, write 1 thing that makes you feel happy. You can write things from the box or other things that make you happy.

pets	reading	books
bikes	drawing	stores
food	swimming	sun
rain	sleeping	walks
family	friends	music

_____

_____

_____

_____

_____

_____

Read the words you wrote in the cup. Then circle **yes** or **no** to answer the questions.

1. Did you write a word that has a short vowel sound?   **yes**   **no**

2. Did you write a word that has a long vowel sound?   **yes**   **no**

3. Did you write a word with a letter pair or blend?   **yes**   **no**

Make a Butterfly Word Catcher

What You Need

- scissors
- glue
- 1 sheet of construction paper

What You Do

1. Pick out four words or phrases from your cup and write one in each circle.

2. Color and cut out the butterfly.

3. Glue it onto a sheet of construction paper. Trim the edges, leaving a border.

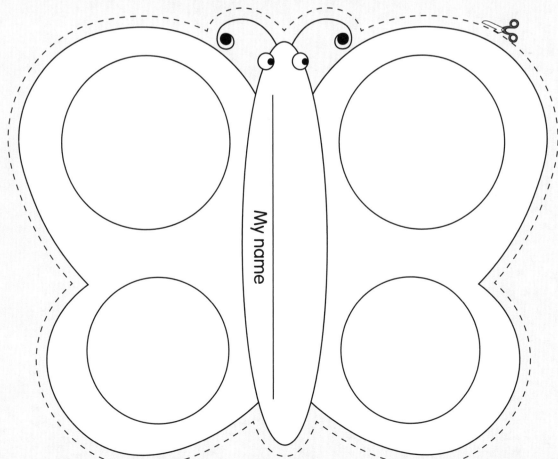

My name

Grammar and Punctuation

Nouns

A **noun** names a person, place, animal, or thing.
Look at the picture. Read the words. Then fill in the
circle next to the noun.

1.

○ run   ○ boy

2.

○ park   ○ open

3.

○ jump   ○ girl

4.

○ book   ○ read

Nouns

A **noun** names a person, place, animal, or thing. Read the sentence. Then underline the common noun, and write it on the line.

1. This is the school.

2. Here is my friend.

3. Where is the cookie?

4. Ask the teacher.

5. The cat ate it.

Nouns Can Name More Than One

Does the noun name **one** or **more than one**?
Circle the correct picture.

1. kites

2. sister

3. rats

4. bird

Add **s** to make the noun name **more than one**.

5. hand_____

7. teacher_____

6. cow_____

8. hat_____

A **plural** noun names **more than one**.
Some plural nouns end in **-es**.
Circle the noun that goes with the picture.

1.   box   boxes

2.   bench   benches

3.   dish   dishes

4.   glass   glasses

5.   dress   dresses

6.   fox   foxes

Add **es** to make the noun name **more than one**.

7. bush_____   **8.** beach_____

Plural Nouns with a Special Spelling

Some plural nouns have a special spelling. Draw a line to match the noun that names **one** to the noun that names **more than one**.

1. goose •   • men

2. mouse •   • teeth

3. child •   • mice

4. man •   • children

5. tooth •   • geese

Read the sentence. Circle the noun or nouns that have a special spelling to name **more than one**.

6. Men and women like to wear hats.

7. Children like to wear hats.

8. Do geese like to wear hats, too?

Plural Nouns with the Same Spelling

Some nouns have the same spelling for **one** and **more than one**. Read the special nouns in the word box. Then write the best word to finish the sentence.

mice   fish   deer   men

1. Five _____ swam in the water.

2. A wild _____ saw the fish.

3. Then three tall _____ sat on a rock.

4. Two tiny _____ saw the men and ran!

Draw a picture to show what the words mean.

5.

five fish	two sheep

Proper Nouns

A **proper noun** names a certain person, place, animal, or thing.
A proper noun begins with a capital letter. Read the sentence.
Then circle the proper nouns.

1. My name is Manny.

2. I live at 344 Main Street.

3. I have a dog named Buddy and a cat named Missy.

4. I wish I lived in a warm city like Houston, Texas.

Read the sentence. The sentences are not correct.
Then write the underlined word or words correctly on the line.

5. My sister's name is <u>kara</u>.

6. She goes to <u>lark school</u>.

Possessive Nouns

A **possessive noun** shows that something belongs to someone or something. Some possessive nouns have an **apostrophe and 's**. Read the sentence. Then circle the possessive noun.

1. Dad's hair is brown.

2. The chair's leg is broken.

3. I like to play at Ben's house.

4. The park's gates are closed.

5. Do you know where Mom's hat is?

6. The bird's wings are long.

7. Did you see Lisa's toy?

Read the sentence. Write the answer.

The cat's tail is long.

8. To whom does the tail belong? _____

Plural Possessives

A possessive noun can be singular or plural.
For **plural nouns** that end in **-s**, write an **apostrophe after the (s')** to make the noun possessive.

1. The trees leaves blow in the wind.

2. The dogs food is in the bowls.

3. Are those the girls books?

4. The cows spots are brown.

- -

Look at the picture. Write the **plural possessive noun** to finish the sentence.

5. The _____ tires are black.

6. The _____ hats look good.

7. The _____ legs are short.

Adjectives

An **adjective** tells about a noun.
Look at the picture. Read the words.
Then fill in the circle next to the adjective.

1.

○ kitten   ○ little

2.

○ three   ○ children

3.

○ hot   ○ boy

4.

○ candy   ○ sweet

Adjectives: How Many and What You See

Some adjectives tell **how many**.

> one   five   many   few   some

Some adjectives tell **how something looks**.

> tall   red   skinny   square

Read the sentence. Then circle the adjective that tells about number, color, or something else you can see.

1. My family planted ten flowers in the garden.

2. The grass in our garden is green.

3. Bright butterflies come to our garden.

4. There are many plants in the garden.

5. Mom put a round rock in the garden.

6. Dad planted yellow tulips.

7. I saw a long worm in the soil!

8. I saw a spotted beetle on a leaf.

Some adjectives tell **how something smells**.

> fresh   stinky   spicy   rotten

Some adjectives tell **how something feels when you touch it**.

> smooth   bumpy   soft   slippery

Read the sentence. Then circle the adjective that tells how something smells or feels when you touch it.

1. My pillow always smells clean.

2. My dog's pillow always smells dirty.

3. My bed is fluffy.

4. My dog's bed is wet.

5. We walk on the trail, and the ocean smells fishy.

6. I like to smell the minty air in my backyard.

7. I throw a squishy toy to my dog.

8. I like to pet my furry dog.

Some adjectives tell **how something sounds**.

loud   quiet   screechy   noisy

Some adjectives tell **how something tastes**.

sweet   salty   creamy   sour

Read the sentence. Then circle the adjective that tells about how something sounds or tastes.

1. The boat has a humming motor.

2. I hear the popping sail in the wind.

3. I chew minty gum as Dad drives the boat.

4. Later, we will eat crunchy trail mix.

5. The moaning boat crashes over a wave.

6. A drop of salty water goes into my mouth.

7. We eat yummy seafood for dinner.

8. I fall asleep to the bubbling sound of the ocean.

Adjectives: What You Feel and Think

Some adjectives tell **how someone feels**.

sad   happy   angry   wishful

Some adjectives tell **what someone thinks** about something or someone else.

cute   funny   mean   nice

Read the sentence. Then circle the adjective that tells about feelings or thoughts.

1. Edwin thinks insects are ugly.

2. Kamala sings a pretty song.

3. Marina says that spiders are scary.

4. The upset baby cries.

5. Joey is excited.

6. Our puppies are playful.

7. It is hard work to care for a pet.

8. It is a wonderful day to go to the beach.

Use Adjectives That End in -er

When you use an adjective, you tell about a noun.
When you add **-er** to the adjective, you are telling how the noun **is different from** another noun. Look at the picture. Then finish the sentence with a word from the box.

> slower   older   shorter   longer   smaller

1. The ruler is _____ than the pencil.

2. My grandpa is _____ than my dad.

3. The snail is _____ than the mouse.

4. My brother is _____ than my sister.

5. A kitten is _____ than an elephant.

Add **-est** to an adjective to tell that it is the **most or least** of something. Read the sentence. Write the best adjective to finish the sentence.

coldest	deepest	quickest
smartest	shortest	longest

1. The _____ boy won the race.

2. The _____ girl got an "A+" on the test.

3. The _____ part of the pool is 8 feet deep.

4. Mom waited in the _____ line at the store.

5. That was the _____ movie we have ever seen!

6. The river is _____ during the winter.

This or That

We use the word **this** to tell about a person, place, animal, or thing that is **nearby**. We use the word **that** to tell about someone or something that is **far away**. Read the sentence. Then write **this** or **that** to finish the sentence.

1. We can stay here at _____ park a little longer.

2. Can you bring me _____ book from the house?

3. _____ apple I am eating tastes sweet.

4. _____ apple the teacher is eating looks juicy.

Write **this** or **that** to finish the rule.

5. Use _____ to tell about someone or something that is **near** you.

6. Use _____ to tell about someone or something that is **far** from you.

These or Those

We use the word **these** to tell about a person, place, animal, or thing that is **nearby**. We use the word **those** to tell about someone or something that is **far away**. Read the sentence. Then write **these** or **those** to finish the sentence.

1. Have you seen _____ freckles on my leg?

2. My mom took _____ pictures I am holding.

3. We looked at _____ books at that library in the city.

4. Dad called _____ people who live in another country.

Write **these** or **those** to finish the rule.

5. Use _____ to tell about people, places, or things that are **near** you.

6. Use _____ to tell about people, places, or things that are **far** from you.

The Words An, A, and The

SKILL
Use articles

We use **a** before adjectives or nouns that name **one**.
The word **a** goes before words that begin with a consonant.
Read the sentence. Circle the word that is wrong.
Then rewrite the sentence with the word **a**.

1. Danny found an crab.

_____

We use **an** before adjectives or nouns that name **one**.
The word **an** goes before words that begin with a vowel.
Read the sentence. Circle the word that is wrong.
Then rewrite the sentence with the word **an**.

2. Deeta steps over a ant.

_____

We use **the** before adjectives or nouns. The nouns can name
one or **more than one**. The word **the** can go before words that
begin with any letter. Read the sentence. Circle the word that
is wrong. Then rewrite the sentence with the word **the**.

3. Latifah sees an hawks flying.

_____

Read the sentence. Then write **a**, **an**, or **the** to finish the sentence.

4. Bill could not finish eating _____ eggs.

Top Student • EMC 9321 • © Evan-Moor Corp.

Personal Pronouns

A **personal pronoun** can take the place of a noun in a sentence. Read the pronouns in the box. Then read the sentence. Last, write a pronoun to take the place of the underlined noun.

> I   you   he   she   it

1. That <u>girl</u> plays soccer.

   _____ plays soccer.

2. <u>Sam</u> plays baseball.

   _____ plays baseball.

3. The children like to play with <u>the ball</u>.

   The children like to play with _____.

Write a sentence with the personal pronoun **I**.

4. _____

   _____

More Personal Pronouns

Read the pronouns in the box. Then read the sentence.
Last, write a pronoun to take the place of the underlined noun.

him	her	we	us	they	them

1. Do you know that boy?

   Do you know _____?

2. His friend Brian eats lunch with Kara and me.

   His friend Brian eats lunch with _____.

3. I think Brian knows those children.

   I think Brian knows _____.

Write a sentence with the personal pronoun **we**.

4. _____

   _____

Possessive Adjectives

A **possessive adjective** tells that something belongs to someone or something. Read the possessive adjectives in the box. Then read the sentences. Last, draw a line to match the sentences.

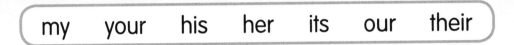

| my | your | his | her | its | our | their |

1. Sara's pencils are sharp. •   • His pencils are sharp.

2. Jake's pencils are sharp. •   • Their pencils are sharp.

3. Drake and Pam's pencils • are sharp.   • Its pencils are sharp.

4. Pedro and your pencils • are sharp.   • Her pencils are sharp.

5. The classroom's pencils • are sharp.   • Our pencils are sharp.

6. Kristin and my pencils • are sharp.   • Your pencils are sharp.

Possessive Pronouns

A **possessive pronoun** tells who or what has something. Read the sentence or sentences. Write a possessive pronoun to take the place of the underlined noun or nouns.

his	hers	ours	theirs	yours	mine

1. <u>Brianna</u> has a pet fish. _____ is named Fin.

2. <u>Sam</u> has two hamsters. _____ are cute.

3. <u>My two fish</u> live in a bowl. The bowl is _____ .

4. Do <u>you</u> feed _____ every day?

5. <u>We</u> feed _____ before we go to school.

Write a sentence with the possessive pronoun **mine**.

6. _____

_____

Other Pronouns

Some pronouns rename nouns.

Clay rides horses.
He rides horses.

Some pronouns do <u>not</u> rename nouns.

Anyone can ride horses.

Read the pronouns in the box.
Then write one to finish each sentence.

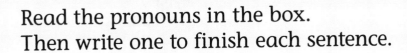

| anyone | everyone | anything | everything |

1. My dad knows _____ about horses.

2. _____ in his family rides horses.

3. I don't know _____ about horses!

4. I don't think _____ in my class rides horses.

5. My dad will teach _____ in my class about horses.

Write a sentence using one of the indefinite pronouns above.

6. _____

_____

Verbs

A **verb** is a word that tells what a noun **does** or **is like**.
Look at the picture, and read the words.
Then fill in the circle next to the verb.

1.

○ reads   ○ girl

2.

○ boy   ○ rides

3.

○ eat   ○ boys

4.

○ children   ○ play

Action Verbs

Some **verbs** tell **action**, or what a noun **does**.
Read the sentence. Look for the action verb.
Then underline the verb in the sentence.

1. The school bell rings.

2. The children stand in line.

3. The teacher opens the door.

4. Noah sits at his desk.

5. Luke reads his book.

6. Karen picks a book.

7. The children listen to their teacher.

8. They play a math game.

9. Paul writes the numbers.

10. Karen and Luke count to one hundred.

Use Is or Are

The verb **is** goes with a singular noun. The verb **are** goes with a plural noun. Read the sentence. Then write **is** or **are** to finish the sentence.

1. The pond _____ a busy place.

2. There _____ many animals to see.

3. The green frogs _____ my favorite.

4. They _____ always jumping.

5. The pond _____ a fun place.

6. There _____ many fish swimming in the water.

7. There _____ one orange fish that swims fast.

8. It _____ the biggest fish in the pond!

Present Tense

A verb can tell **what is happening now**. Read the sentence.
Then write the verb that tells what is happening now.

1. I _____ Dad on the phone.
   call   **called**

2. I _____ him to buy apples.
   ask   **asked**

3. Dad _____ okay.
   says   **said**

4. Mom says she _____ green apples.
   wants   **wanted**

5. Dad _____ the apples.
   buys   **bought**

6. Mom _____ an apple pie.
   makes   **made**

Write a sentence that tells about something **happening now**.

7. _____

_____

Past Tense

A verb can tell **what already happened**. Look at the pictures. Then finish each sentence with a verb from the box.

roared   followed   moved   waved   clapped

1.  The men _____ the tents.

2. 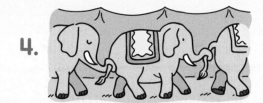 The lion _____ loudly.

3.  The people _____.

4.  The elephants _____ each other.

5.  The clowns _____ at the crowd.

Future Tense

A verb can tell **what will happen in the future**.
We use the word **will** with the verb to tell about
an action that will happen. Read the sentences.
Finish each sentence. Write **will** and the verb
to tell what will happen in the future.

1. Lana _____ her bed.
   make

2. She _____ her teeth.
   brush

3. Ken _____ his shoes.
   tie

4. He _____ his lunch.
   pack

5. Mom _____ us to school.
   drive

Write a sentence. Use **will** and a verb
to tell about something that **will happen
in the future**.

6. _____

   _____

Prepositions

A **preposition** is a word that connects a noun or pronoun to another word in a sentence. Look at the picture. Read the sentence. Then fill in the circle next to the preposition.

1.

The dog is in the house.

○ dog   ○ in

2.

The cat is behind the box.

○ behind   ○ cat

3.

They are under the umbrella.

○ They   ○ under

4.

She sits on the bike.

○ on   ○ She

Joining Words

Some words are **joining words**. They connect other words in a sentence. Read the sentence. Then write a joining word from the box to finish the sentence.

| and | but | or | so | because |

1. I woke up late _____ it was Saturday.
   because   or

2. Mom made pancakes _____ eggs.
   but   and

3. After I ate, I wanted to skate _____ ride my bike.
   or   so

4. I put on my bike helmet, _____ then it started to rain!
   so   but

Write a sentence with the word **because**.

5. _____

_____

_____

_____

End Marks

Every sentence needs an **end mark**.
A sentence that **tells something** ends with a **period** [.].
A sentence that **asks something** ends with a **question mark** [?].

Read the sentence that tells about something. Then write a sentence of your own that **tells about something**.

1. I like to read books about animals.

_____

_____

_____

Read the sentence that asks a question. Then write a sentence of your own that **asks a question**.

2. Did you do your homework?

_____

_____

_____

Write End Marks

A sentence that **shows excitement or strong feelings** ends with an **exclamation point** !.

Read the sentence that shows excitement. Then write a sentence of your own that **shows excitement**.

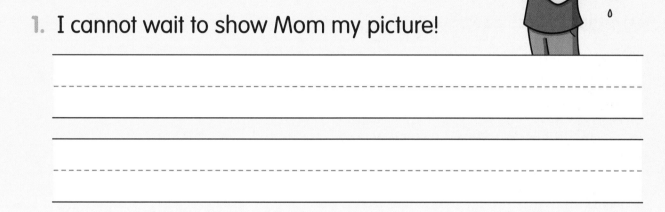

1. I cannot wait to show Mom my picture!

_____

- -

_____

- -

_____

Read the sentence. Then write a **period**, **question mark**, or **exclamation point** at the end.

2. My grandpa is the best_____

3. We learn about the weather_____

4. What kinds of birds migrate_____

5. I am so excited to go on the ride_____

Commas in Dates

We write a **comma** , between the day and the year in a date.
Write commas where they belong in the sentences below.

1. Jamal's birthday party is on March 24 2022.

2. Tanya got Jamal a gift on March 20 2022.

3. Marie's birthday is on April 17 2022.

4. Marie might have a party on April 19 2022.

5. Her little brother Jared turns 2 on July 6 2022.

6. Jamal's little sister turns 4 on September 3 2022.

Write today's date. Use a comma.

7. _____

Write the date you were born.
Use a comma.

8. _____

MARCH

Sunday	Monday	Tuesday	Wednesday	Thursday	Friday	Saturday
1	2	3	4	5	6	7
8	9	10	11	12	13	14
15	16	17	18	19	20	21
22	23	24	25	26	27	28
29	30	31				

Capital Letters Begin Sentences

All sentences begin with a **capital letter**. Read the sentence. Find the mistake. Rewrite the word that needs a capital letter.

1. the movie is starting.

   _____

2. do you know who is making popcorn?

   _____

3. please ask Mike to call me.

   _____

Write a sentence about your friend.

4. _____

Days of the Week

Each day of the week begins with a **capital letter**.
Write the days of the week in order. Begin each day
with a capital letter.

1. _____

2. _____

3. _____

4. _____

5. _____

6. _____

7. _____

Sunday
Monday
Tuesday
Wednesday
Thursday
Friday
Saturday

Write a day of the week to finish the sentence.

8. Today is _____.

Names of Months

Write the months of the year correctly

Each month of the year begins with a **capital letter**.
Read the sentences. Find the mistake.
Rewrite the word that needs a capital letter.

1. It rains a lot in april.

_____

2. It is sunny and hot in july.

_____

3. I hope it snows in december!

_____

Write a sentence about your favorite month.

4. _____

_____

_____

© Evan-Moor Corp. • EMC 9321 • Top Student

97

Can I Be a Noun or an Adjective or a Verb?

SKILLS
Social and Emotional Learning: Evaluate your feelings; Demonstrate self-awareness

Write a word to finish each sentence about yourself.
You can use words from the boxes or your own words.

Adjectives	
smart	strong
angry	friendly
helpful	happy
brave	fair

Nouns	
hero	grouch
friend	star
neighbor	person
moaner	helper

Verbs	
complain	help
share	fight
play	talk
clean	exercise

1. I am a _____ when I help others.
   noun

2. I feel _____ when I try my hardest to do a job.
   adjective

3. I am happy when I _____ with others.
   verb

4. I am a _____ person when I tell the truth.
   adjective

5. I am a _____ when I am not nice to others.
   noun

Top Student • EMC 9321 • © Evan-Moor Corp.

Spelling and Vocabulary

Short and Long Sounds: a

SKILLS
Discriminate short and long a vowel sounds;
Categorize short and long a words

Group the words by **short a** and **long a** vowel sounds.
First, read a spelling word. Listen for the vowel sound.
Then write the word in the correct box.

1.

Spelling Words

sand	make	had	came
game	hand	lake	shake
ran	late	tape	pat

ate	hat
_____ _____	_____ _____
_____ _____	_____ _____
_____ _____	_____ _____
_____ _____	_____ _____

Change one letter to make a spelling word.

2. bake   ____ake

3. cape   ____ape

4. same   ____ame

5. sat   ____at

Short and Long Sounds: e

SKILLS
Discriminate short and long e vowel sounds:
Categorize short and long e words

Group the words by **short e** and **long e** vowel sounds.
First, read a word. Listen for the vowel sound.
Then write the word in the correct box.

1.

Spelling Words

fed	we	me	red	need
he	bee	tree	see	free
ten	get	let	men	bed

be	pet
_____ _____	_____ _____
_____ _____	_____ _____
_____ _____	_____ _____
_____ _____	_____ _____

Write to complete each rhyming word.

2. Who will <u>be</u> there with m_____?

3. This is the <u>seed</u> that I will n_____.

4. Can you <u>see</u> that big t_____?

5. I can <u>keep</u> the white s_____!

Short and Long Sounds: i and y

SKILLS
Discriminate short and long i vowel sounds;
Categorize short and long i words

Group the words by **short i** and **long i** vowel sounds.
First, read a spelling word. Listen for the vowel sound.
Then write the word in the correct box.

1.

Spelling Words				
it	dime	pig	like	by
big	did	nine	five	his
ride	sit	six	dig	time

dive	is
_____ _____	_____ _____
_____ _____	_____ _____
_____ _____	_____ _____
_____ _____	_____ _____

Change one letter to make a spelling word.

2. hive   ____ive

3. bike   ____ike

4. lime   ____ime

5. my   ____y

6. side   ____ide

7. mine   ____ine

Short and Long Sounds: O

SKILLS
Discriminate short and long o vowel sounds;
Categorize short and long o words

Group the words by **short o** and **long o** vowel sounds.
First, read a spelling word. Listen for the vowel sound.
Then write the word in the correct box.

1.

Spelling Words

not	dog	go	so	mop
hop	home	on	top	
note	fox	robe	stop	

no	hot
_____ _____	_____ _____
_____ _____	_____ _____
_____ _____	_____ _____
_____	_____ _____

Change one letter to make a spelling word.

2. no   _____o

3. vote   _____ote

4. dome   _____ome

5. lobe   _____obe

Short and Long Sounds: U

SKILLS
Discriminate short and long u vowel sounds;
Categorize short and long u words

Group the words by **short u** and **long u** vowel sounds.
First, read a spelling word. Listen for the vowel sound.
Then write the word in the correct box.

1.

Spelling Words

cut	shut	rude	tube	stuff
chute	duck	stuck	Luke	tub
run	rule	fuss	tune	

flute	but
_____ _____	_____ _____
_____ _____	_____ _____
_____ _____	_____ _____
_____	_____

Unscramble the letters to write the **short u** word.

pup   bus   but   tub

2. ppu   _____

3. btu   _____

4. bsu   _____

5. tbu   _____

Spell Correctly: -ll

Read the words in the box.
Then write letters to finish the words.

Spelling Words

hill   bell   fell   ball   fall

1. 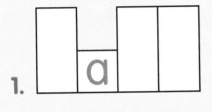 a

2. 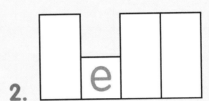 e

3. 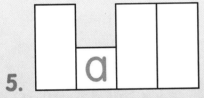 i

4. 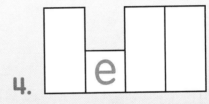 e

5. a

Unscramble the letters. Write the spelling words.

6. lihl _____

7. labl _____

8. elbl _____

9. flle _____

10. albl _____

11. lleb _____

12. allf _____

13. elfl _____

14. illh _____

Spell Correctly: sh- and -sh

Read the words in the box.
Then write letters to finish the words.

Spelling Words

she   ship   shell   dish   wish

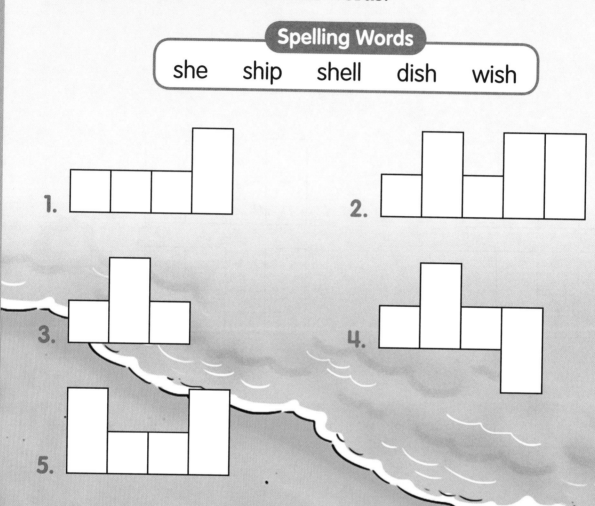

1.

2.

3.

4.

5.

Draw a circle around each spelling word.

shipsh   shwish   shesh

shellsh   shdish   shship

shshe   wishsh   shshell

Find Misspelled Words

SKILL
Identify correctly spelled words

Read the words in the row.
Then circle the word that is spelled correctly.

1. five   fif

2. lik   like

3. ride   ryde

4. mi   my

5. mak   make

6. lake   lak

7. came   kame

8. game   gaem

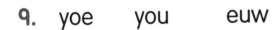

9. yoe   you   euw

10. do   du   doo

11. roob   robbe   robe

12. noot   note   nowt

13. home   howm   hom

14. nw   noo   no

15. sw   su   so

16. go   gw   gow

Is It Spelled Correctly?: Double Consonants

SKILL
Spell words with double consonants

Read the ending letters in the box.
Then write ending letters to finish each word.

> nny   ppy   tten

1. bu_____

2. mi_____

3. ha_____

4. ki_____

5. fu_____

6. pe_____

7. A baby cat is called a _____.

8. A baby rabbit is called a _____.

9. A baby dog is called a _____.

Unscramble the letters.
Write the spelling words.

> **Spelling Words**
> funny   bunny   penny   happy   mitten   little

10. eynnp _____

11. eimntt _____

12. uybnn _____

13. ayhpp _____

14. uyfnn _____

15. tiltel _____

What's the New Word?

SKILLS
Write CVC words; Draw to illustrate a word

Change the first letter in the word to make another word. Then write it and draw a picture of the new word.

1. mat

___at

2. big

___ig

3. tin

___in

4. pen

___en

5. pup

___up

6. hop

___op

Spell a New Word

Change one letter in the word to make another word.
Then write the new word on the line and draw a picture of it.

1. bat

_____

2. top

_____

3. day

_____

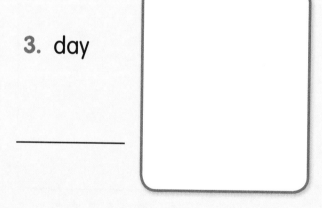

4. mug

_____

5. hot

_____

6. win

_____

Write Compound Words

A **compound word** is made from two shorter words. Read the two words. Then write them together as one word.

1. sun + flower = _____

2. base + ball = _____

3. air + plane = _____

4. play + ground = _____

5. back + pack = _____

Write the compound word that names the picture.

6. _____   7. _____

8. _____

Find Compound Words

Read the sentence. Then circle the compound word.

1. My friends and I like to play baseball.

2. We like to be in the sunshine.

3. We sit down and eat some cupcakes.

4. We see a butterfly sit on a flower.

5. Its colors look like a rainbow.

6. We watch a firefly go by.

7. It has an orange glow like a goldfish.

8. It is fun to play in the backyard.

Write a sentence with a compound word.

9. _____

_____

Homophones

Homophones are words that sound alike, but they have different meanings. Look at the picture. Then circle the correct homophone.

1.

cent

sent

2.

sail

sale

3.

pair

pear

4.

bee

be

5.

won

one

6.

to

two

Synonyms

Synonyms are words that have almost the same meaning.
Read the word. Then write synonyms from the word box.

huge	kind	chuckle	angry
upset	giggle	caring	large

1. big

_____

_____

2. nice

_____

_____

3. laugh

_____

_____

4. mad

_____

_____

Antonyms

Antonyms are words that have opposite meanings.
Draw a line to match each word with its antonym.

1. soft • • hard

2. big • • slow

3. fast • • little

4. more • • old

5. dark • • less

6. young • • light

Look at the pictures.
Finish each sentence with
an antonym from above.

7. The man is _____.

   The boy is _____.

8. The man is sitting on a _____ chair.

   The boy is sitting on a _____ rock.

Words I Know

Read the question. Circle the best answer.
Then write another word of your own to answer the question.

1. What makes you feel <u>warm</u>?

   apple   paper   socks   _____

2. What makes you feel <u>cold</u>?

   shoes   rain   banana   _____

3. What feels <u>soft</u>?

   crayon   cookie   blanket   _____

4. What feels <u>hard</u>?

   rock   ball   orange   _____

5. What feels <u>smooth</u>?

   sand   bird   grape   _____

6. What feels <u>crunchy</u>?

   milk   cracker   tomato   _____

7. What feels <u>wet</u>?

   soup   bat   pencil   _____

Top Student • EMC 9321 • © Evan-Moor Corp.

Sort Words

Words can be sorted into groups. Read the words in the box.
Then write each word under the group it belongs in.

| doctor | mouse | sister | lion |
| bird | baby | dog | teacher |

1.

People

_____

_____

_____

Animals

_____

_____

_____

Write another word to go in the **Animals** group.

2. _____

Matching Words to Their Meanings

Read the words.
Draw a line to match.

1. A bird that swims   •

2. A small green animal that hops   •

3. An animal that has fins and swims   •

• frog

• duck

• fish

Read the words.
Draw a line to match.

4. cow   •

5. pig   •

6. horse   •

• A farm animal with a curly tail

• A farm animal that gives us milk

• A farm animal to ride on

118

Shades of Meaning

Some words have almost the same meaning, but the meanings are a little bit different. Read the first two words in the row. Then write the word that has almost the same meaning.

1. tap, knock, _____

   pound   **yell**

2. peek, look, _____

   stare   **write**

3. skip, jog, _____

   wash   **run**

4. hop, jump, _____

   sit   **leap**

5. hum, chant, _____

   sing   **dance**

Finding the Meaning of New Words

Some words have almost the same meaning, but the meanings are a little bit different. Read the first two words in the row. Then write the word that has almost the same meaning.

1. glad,   happy,   _____
   warm   thrilled

2. big,   giant,   _____
   thin   huge

3. tiny,   little,   _____
   small   round

4. good,   great,   _____
   wonderful   cool

5. bad,   terrible,   _____
   loud   awful

HOME 4 GUEST
12 INNING 08

Use Word Clues

Read the sentences. What do the bold words mean?
The underlined words are **clues**.
Write the meanings of the bold words.

1. Dan was so **worn out** that he <u>lay down and fell asleep</u>.

   Worn out means _____.

             hungry   tired

2. The <u>sleepy</u> firefighters **awoke** to a loud alarm.

   Awoke means _____.

           woke up   ran

3. The **sturdy** tree had <u>many branches</u> and leaves.

   Sturdy means _____.

          weak   strong

4. A cactus plant grows in the <u>sandy</u> **desert**.

   Desert means _____.

         dry land   wet land

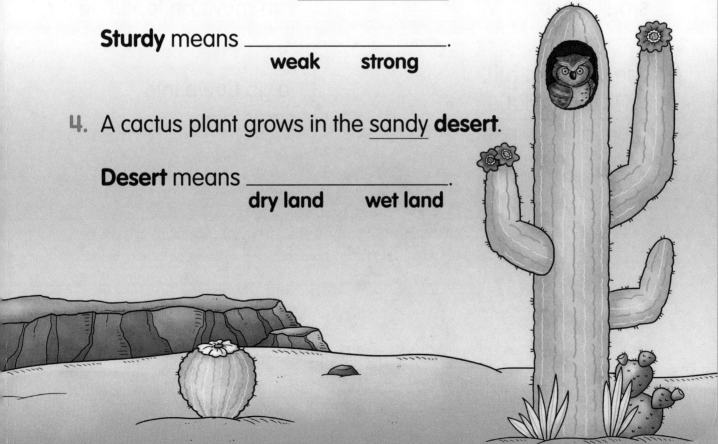

Word Clues Help You Know the Meaning

Read the sentence. What does the bold word mean?
Use the words in the sentence as a **clue**. Then draw a line
to match the sentence to the meaning of the bold word.

1. The children take turns going down the long red **slide**. •   • to cut into pieces

2. The girl's rain boot started to **sink** into the mud. •   • having as much or as many as can fit

3. Mom **chops** the fruit into many small pieces. •   • a smooth object on a playground that people can move on top of easily

4. The basket is **full**, so I cannot put more apples in it. •   • to go down into something

122

Vocabulary Practice

Read the sentence. Draw a line from the sentence to the meaning of the bold word.

1. A famous **singer** is on the stage.

2. She sang a **cheerful** song.

3. The **careless** driver dented his car.

4. The **baker** made cookies and pies.

5. The bike is **useless** with its flat tire.

6. The **fearless** man went up the mountain.

7. The **helpful** coach taught us the rules.

• without care

• a person who sings

• full of cheer

• a person who bakes

• without fear

• without use

• full of help

Base Words

Read the words. Draw a line to the base word.

1. opens, opened, opening ●   ● talk

2. cooks, cooked, cooking ●   ● cook

3. talks, talked, talking ●   ● open

4. cleans, cleaned, cleaning ●   ● start

5. plays, played, playing ●   ● play

6. starts, started, starting ●   ● clean

7. yells, yelled, yelling ●   ● look

8. looks, looked, looking ●   ● yell

Words I Can Use

Read the paragraph. Think about what the bold word means.

> The **cute** kittens were so little! They had little eyes, ears, and mouths. They rolled across the floor and meowed softly for their mother.

Write a sentence about something or someone in your own life who is **cute**.

1. _____

_____

> My mom wears **fancy** clothes on holidays. She has one dress that is long and red. It has small diamonds that shine when she moves. She wears big gold earrings and a diamond necklace, too.

Write a sentence about something in your own life that is **fancy**.

2. _____

_____

Words to Show Who You Are!

SKILLS
Social and Emotional Learning:
Demonstrate self-awareness; Evaluate your feelings; Draw to express yourself

Words are important. We use words to tell how we feel and what we think. Use words and pictures to tell about yourself. Follow the steps below.

1. Draw your eyes on the face.

2. Draw your nose and mouth on the face.

3. Draw a hat that you would like to wear.

4. On the hat, write a word that tells how you feel.

5. On the forehead, write a word that tells something you are good at.

6. On the chin, write a word that tells something you love.

Reading

Put Steps in Order

Look at the pictures of Lindsey washing her hair.
Write the number **1**, **2**, **3**, or **4** in the box next to
each picture to show the order of steps Lindsey follows.

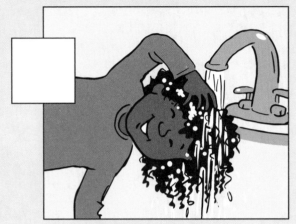

I rinse my hair.

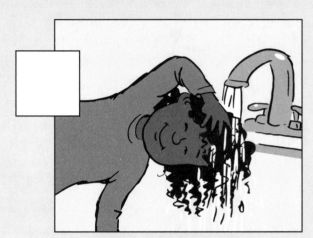

I wet my hair.

I put in shampoo.

I need to wash my hair.

Now write the steps in order.

1. _____

2. _____

3. _____

4. _____

First, Next, and Last

Some texts tell when things happen.
Read. Then answer the items.

> **How to Plant a New Tree**
>
> First, dig a hole.
> Next, put the tree in the hole.
> Last, put dirt around the tree.

1. Write the sentence that tells what to do **first**.

   _____

   _____

2. Write the sentence that tells what to do **last**.

   _____

   _____

3. Why is it important to tell when things happen?

   _____

   _____

   _____

Sequence

Some texts tell when things happen.
The texts can tell what happens **first**, **next**, and **last**.
Read the text below. Then answer the items.

Sea turtles live in warm water. They can swim very far. Lots of sea turtles stay in the water all the time. But sometimes, mother sea turtles come out of the water and go on land. Mother sea turtles lay eggs on land. Baby sea turtles are born on land.

First, the mother sea turtle digs a hole in the sand. **Next**, she lays eggs in the hole. **Last**, baby sea turtles come out of the eggs.

Later, the baby sea turtles go into the water with the other sea turtles.

The baby sea turtles are going into the water.

Top Student • EMC 9321 • © Evan-Moor Corp.

Answer the items about the text you read.

1. What does a mother sea turtle do **first** when
she goes on land to lay eggs?

   ○ The baby sea turtles come out of the eggs.

   ○ The mother sea turtle digs a hole in the sand.

2. What happens **next**?
The mother sea turtle _____.

3. What do baby sea turtles do after they are born?

   _____

4. Draw a picture of a baby sea turtle in the water.

Baby Sea Turtle Art

You just read about baby sea turtles. Think about how they look. You will make a baby sea turtle.

What You Need

- scissors
- glue or glue stick
- green marker, crayon, or colored pencil
- paper plate
- cutouts on pages 133 and 135

What You Do

1. Cut out the turtle shell on page 133.

2. Glue the turtle shell onto the back of the paper plate. Color any parts of the paper plate that are sticking out green.

3. Cut out the turtle body parts on page 135.

4. Glue the head, tail, and legs to the paper plate so they stick out and look like a turtle.

Now your turtle is done!

Top Student • EMC 9321 • © Evan-Moor Corp.

Read these fun facts about sea turtles, and tell them to someone.

Fun Facts

- Sea turtles' favorite food is jellyfish.
- Sea turtles have been on Earth for 110 million years.
- Sea turtles can hold their breath for 5 hours under water.

Turtle Shell

turtle head

front legs

Glue

Glue

Glue

back legs

Glue

Glue

tail

Glue

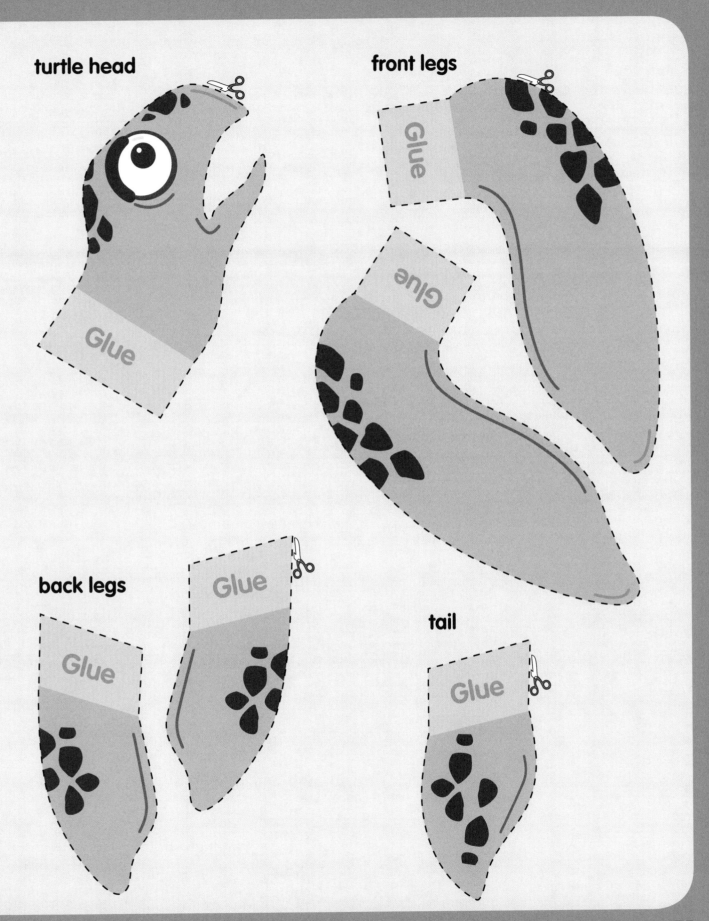

Top Student • EMC 9321 • © Evan-Moor Corp.

Real or Make-Believe?

Look at the picture. Could it really happen?
Circle **yes** or **no**. Then write to tell why.

1.

_____

_____

_____

_____

_____

yes   no

2.

_____

_____

_____

_____

_____

yes   no

The Ant's Voice, A Tale from East Africa

Read the story. Then answer the items.

Once upon a time an ant needed a new house. The ant saw a cave. No one was home. The ant went into the cave. Then a lizard came home to the cave. The lizard saw tracks. "Who is in my house?" she called.

The ant's voice boomed from the cave. "It is I! I am strong enough to crush an elephant. Who dares to ask?" The lizard ran away.

The lizard asked a warthog for help. The warthog stood outside the cave. "Who is in my friend's house?" he barked.

The ant's voice boomed from the cave. "It is I! I am strong enough to crush an elephant. Who dares to ask?" The warthog ran away.

The lizard asked a little frog for help. The frog stood in the cave opening. "I am strong enough to crush anyone who can crush an elephant!" croaked the frog in a big voice.

The ant shook when he saw the frog's big shadow. "I have had my fun," said the ant. And the ant ran right out of the cave!

SKILLS
Discriminate between real and make-believe;
Demonstrate reading comprehension

Answer items about the story.
Fill in the circle to finish each sentence.

1. The story of the ant's voice is _____.

   ○ true

   ○ made up

2. The animals in the story _____.

   ○ talk

   ○ sing

3. The _____ fooled some of the other animals.

   ○ lizard

   ○ ant

4. The _____ fooled the ant.

   ○ frog

   ○ elephant

We Need the Sun

Read the text. Then answer the items.

The sun helps us.
The sun gives us light and heat.
The heat keeps us warm.
The world would be as cold as ice
without the sun.

The light from the sun helps us see.
Children play outside when the
sun shines. People have picnics
at the park when the sun shines.

The sun helps plants and
animals, too. The sun's light
helps plants grow. Animals
eat plants for food.

People eat plants, too.
People eat food from animals.
Plants, animals, and people
need the sun to live.

Top Student • EMC 9321 • © Evan-Moor Corp.

Answer the items about the text you read.

1. Who or what needs the sun to live?
   ○ rocks, toys, and water
   ○ people, plants, and animals

2. How do you feel when the sun is not shining?

   _____

3. Draw a picture of one thing that you like to do in the sun.

Look at the picture. Read the words.
Then answer the question.

1. This sign is at the park.

   What does this sign ask
   people to do?

   _____

   _____

2. This child is at the zoo.

   What do you think the sign
   says at this zoo?

   ○ Do Not Feed the Animals
   ○ You May Feed the Animals

Answer the question.

3. What can words and pictures on a sign tell you?
   ○ They help you know what to do.
   ○ They tell you a story.

Read and look at the pictures.
Then answer the questions.

How many legs does each living thing have?

| An insect has 6 legs. | A spider has 8 legs. | A gorilla has 2 legs. | A lion has 4 legs. |

1. What do the pictures show?

   ○ They show how many legs each living thing has.

   ○ They show the name of each living thing.

2. Do the pictures tell about the words?

   ○ yes

   ○ no

Batri's New Friend

Read the story. Look at the pictures carefully.
Then answer the items.

Batri's New Friend

Batri likes to do fun things.
Batri likes to play every day.
Batri likes to play ball. Batri
likes to go on the swings.

Batri likes to ride a bike.
But Batri needs a friend to play with.

One day, Batri's mom came
home with a new friend for Batri.
Batri's new friend has soft, white fur.
Batri's new friend has a wet, pink nose.
Batri's new friend makes a silly sound
when it drinks milk. Batri's new friend
likes to eat fish.

Batri is having so much fun
with her new friend. Now Batri
wants more friends to play with!

LAP!
LAP!
LAP!

Top Student • EMC 9321 • © Evan-Moor Corp.

SKILLS
Demonstrate reading comprehension;
Demonstrate visual literacy; Make inferences

Answer the items about the story you read.
Look at the pictures as you answer.

1. Batri is a _____.

   ○ girl

   ○ boy

2. Batri's new friend is a _____.

   ○ mouse

   ○ cat

Answer the items.

3. Who does Batri play with before the new friend?
   Tell how you know.

   _____

   _____

4. Write two other animals that Batri could be friends with.

   _____

   _____

Pictures Help Us Understand

Read the story, and look at the picture.
Use clues in the picture to answer the questions.

Brian played on his sled all day. He was tired. His sled was hard to pull home. Suddenly, his sled was easy to pull.

1. Why did the sled suddenly become easy to pull?

_____

_____

2. What clue did you use?

_____

_____

Sentences That Do Not Belong

SKILLS
Demonstrate reading comprehension;
Identify unrelated sentences

A paragraph should be about one thing. Read each paragraph. Look at the picture. Then cross out the sentence in the paragraph that does <u>not</u> belong.

1.

I take care of animals. I give them food and water. I have long hair. The animals are safe with me.

2.

I work at a school. I help kids read. I have a sick pet at home. My students love to learn.

3.

It is warm outside. We like to work on computers. We solve problems. We work as a team.

Main Idea

A **main idea** is what a text is mostly about.
Read each paragraph below.
Then answer the question about the paragraph.

1.　　Sea otters eat a lot of different foods. They like to eat crabs. They like to eat fish. They like to eat frogs. Sea otters love to eat.

What is the text mostly about?

○ Sea otters live in the sea.

○ Sea otters eat a lot of different foods.

2.　　Some fish are big. Some fish are small. Some have stripes and dots. There are many kinds of fish in the sea.

What is the main idea of the text?

_____

_____

Clues to Find the Main Idea

A paragraph has a **main idea**. You can look for words that are in the paragraph more than once. They can help you know the main idea. Read the paragraph. Then answer the items.

Some bugs help plants. A stinkbug eats smaller bugs that eat plants. The stinkbug is a bug that helps plants stay big and strong. A bee moves pollen from flower to flower. This bug helps make more flowers.

1. Write the sentence that tells you the main idea.

   _____

2. Which sentence tells more about the main idea?
    ○ A stinkbug eats smaller bugs that eat plants.
    ○ A stinkbug is red with black dots.

3. Write words that you see more than once.

   _____   _____   _____

A Story Can Tell What's the Same and What's Different

SKILLS
Demonstrate reading comprehension;
Compare and contrast characters in a text

When you read a story, you can think about what is the **same** and what is **different**. Read the story below. Then answer the items.

Terrell and Pete are best friends. Terrell likes the color red. Pete likes the color green. Terrell likes to play with cards. Pete likes to play soccer. Terrell and Pete both like to eat apples. They are both in first grade.

1. This story tells how Terrell and Pete are _____.
   - ○ the same
   - ○ different
   - ○ the same and different

2. Write one way that Terrell and Pete are the **same**.

   _____

3. Write one way that Terrell and Pete are **different**.

   _____

   _____

Same or Different?

Read. Then mark **same** or **different**.

1. Morgan has a blanket, but Dora does not.
   ○ same   ○ different

2. My hamster and my cat both have tan fur.
   ○ same   ○ different

3. Tatum wants to go to the park. Audrey wants to go, too.
   ○ same   ○ different

Read. Then draw a picture of Sam's and Pat's teddy bears.

4.   Sam's teddy bear has a circle belly button. Pat's teddy bear has a heart belly button. Both teddy bears have ears, but they are different. Sam's bear has big ears, but Pat's bear has small ears.

Ducks and Chickens

A text can tell how things are the **same** and **different**. Read the text. Then answer the items.

Ducks and Chickens

Ducks and chickens are birds.
Ducks have feathers like chickens do.
Both ducks and chickens can fly.
Chickens lay eggs, and ducks do, too.
When the eggs hatch, little baby birds come out!

But ducks are different from chickens.
A baby duck is called a duckling.
A baby chicken is called a chick.
A chicken has a pointed beak.
A duck has a flat bill instead of a pointed beak. A chicken has sharp toes on its feet.

Chickens use their beaks and feet to dig up food in the ground. But ducks find food in the water. They have webbed feet. They use their webbed feet to swim.

Ducks and chickens are the same in some ways. But they are also different in some ways.

SKILLS
Demonstrate reading comprehension; Write
to compare and contrast

The text tells how ducks and chickens are the same
and different. Answer the items about the text.

1. Write how ducks and chickens are the **same**.

_____

_____

2. Write how chickens are **different** from ducks.

_____

_____

Draw a line to show who the feet belong to.

3.

duck  •   •

chicken  •   •

Cause and Effect

SKILLS
Demonstrate reading comprehension;
Identify cause and effect in a text

★ An **effect** is something that happens.
A **cause** is the reason why it happens.

CAUSE The sun went down.

EFFECT The sky is dark.

Many things can be a cause or an effect.

Read. Then answer the items.

The clouds are gray and thick, so it is going to rain. You can see a rainbow in the sky when the sun shines in the rain.

1. It rains because ____.
   - ○ there is a rainbow in the sky
   - ○ the clouds are gray and thick

2. Mark the **cause** in the box.

effect		cause
You can see a rainbow in the sky	**because**	○ The sun shines in the rain. ○ The sun shines on clouds.

Tell Why It Happens

SKILLS
Demonstrate reading comprehension;
Answer cause-and-effect questions

Read. Then answer the questions.

> The lake is made of water.
> When the air is very cold,
> the water turns to ice.
> Children skate on the lake
> when it turns to ice.

1. Why does the water turn to ice?

   ○ The sun shines.

   ○ The air is very cold.

2. What happens when the lake water turns to ice?

   ○ Children swim in the lake.

   ○ Children skate on the lake.

3. What is the water like when it turns to ice?

   ○ It is hard.

   ○ It is soft.

Beach Fun

A story can tell about **cause and effect**. Things in the story happen. Then those things can make other things happen. Read the story. Then answer the items.

Beach Fun

When Aspen woke up, the sun was shining. "If you clean your room, we can go to the beach," said Aspen's mom. Aspen got out of bed and put away her toys.

At the beach, she put her toes in the water. She also made shapes in the sand. Aspen saw a crab by her. "Hello, Crab," said Aspen.

"Can you help clean my beach?" asked the crab. Aspen saw lots of cans and litter on the beach. She wanted to help. So she picked up the litter. Then she put it into bins. The crab helped clean up, too.

Soon, the beach was clean. The crab was very happy. And so was Aspen.

SKILLS
Demonstrate reading comprehension;
Answer cause-and-effect questions; Draw to
show comprehension

Answer the items about the story you read.

1. Why did Aspen clean her room?

   _____

2. Why did the crab talk to Aspen?

   _____

3. What made the crab happy?

   _____

4. Draw how the beach looked after Aspen helped to clean it.

   ┌───┐
   │   │
   │   │
   │   │
   │   │
   │   │
   │   │
   │   │
   │   │
   └───┘

What You Read Can Be a Clue!

When you read, you can figure out something the author didn't write. You can use clues in the words and pictures. Read and look at the pictures below. Then answer the items.

1.  This drops from clouds. It fills lakes. It helps plants grow. It is _____.

    ○ rain

    ○ wind

2.  The children are wearing mittens and a big coat. The weather outside is _____.

    ○ warm

    ○ cold

Finish the sentence.

3. The weather person says it is cold today.

    I think it is _____ outside.
    cloudy   sunny

Read Closely

Read and look at the picture.
Use clues in the story and the picture to finish the sentence.

1.

Bozy barks. He sniffs his bowl. He pushes the bowl close to my feet. He sits by his bowl and wags his tail.

Bozy wants _____.

○ to go for a walk

○ food in his bowl

2.

Ben just got home. He shows his mom a shell. He shows her what is in his bucket.

Ben was at the _____.

○ beach

○ park

3.

Tyson's mom made a cake for him. Tyson is 7 years old now. His friends are going to come to his house later. They will sing to him.

Today is _____.

○ the first day of school

○ Tyson's birthday

Key Details in a Text

SKILLS
Demonstrate reading comprehension;
Identify key details in a text

Read. Then answer the questions.

> Snails do not have bones. They can live on land or in water. A snail has a hard shell. It can pull its body inside its shell. The shell keeps the snail safe. A snail has a soft body and one long foot. A snail makes a trail of slime when it moves.

1. What is the text about?

   ○ shells   ○ snails

2. What happens when a snail moves?

   _____

3. Why does a snail pull its body inside its shell?

   _____

   _____

Write a Title

Read what each book is about. Then write a title for each book. Write a title that gives a clue about the book's topic.

1.

   Anna loves baseball. She hits a home run every time she uses her special bat. Today, she forgot her bat at home.

2. Joe and I love bugs. We dig in the dirt to find them. Joe's favorite is the ladybug. My favorite is the ant.

3.

   Frank wants to be a fireman when he grows up. On his birthday, he gets to go to the fire station! He will see how everything works.

Does the Sentence Tell About Me?

SKILLS
Social and Emotional Learning: Demonstrate
self-reflection; Evaluate your feelings

Read the sentence. Color the 😊 if the sentence tells about you.
Color the ☹ if the sentence does not tell about you.

I care about other people's feelings.	😊	☹
I do not like it when other people are nice to me.	😊	☹
I am good at lots of things.	😊	☹
I am not good at anything.	😊	☹

All people have needs. Read the words.
Color the circles with words that tell what you **need**.

water   sleep   food   clothes   hugs

Writing

Facts About Me

Write to finish the sentences.
Then draw your face and hair on the child.

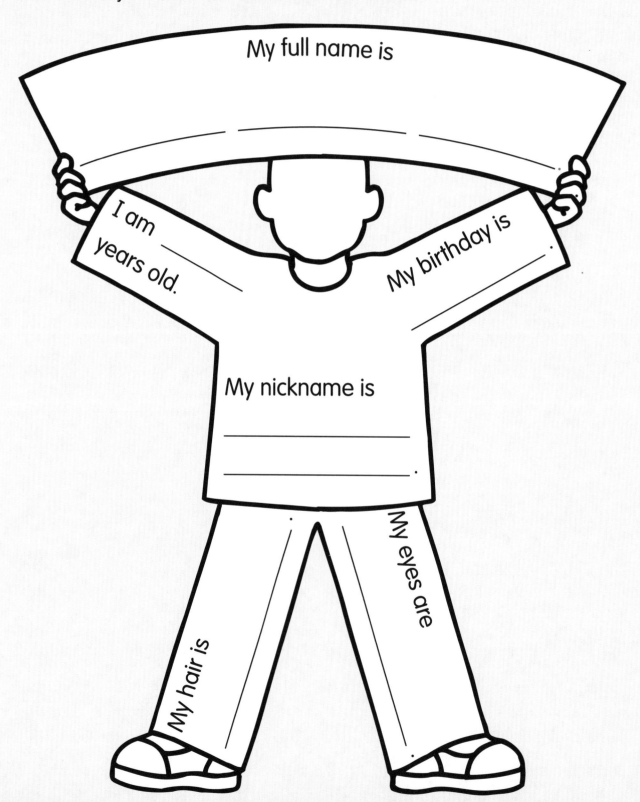

My full name is

I am _____ years old.

My birthday is

My nickname is

My eyes are

My hair is

Write a List

Write a list of 3 fruits you like to eat.

1. _____

2. _____

3. _____

Write a list of 3 rooms in your house.

4. _____

5. _____

6. _____

Words Can Tell About Pictures

Look at the picture. Then answer the items.

1. Circle the **noun** that tells what or who is in the picture.

   class   family   shop

2. Circle the **adjective** that tells about the people in the picture.

   afraid   sad   happy

Look at the picture. Read the words in the box.
Then write an adjective from the box to finish the sentence.

3.

hot   yellow   round

Her snowball is _____.

Make a Sentence

Finish the sentence.
Write a word or words from the box.

> laughs   barks   The girl   The kids

1. _____ tells a joke.

2. The boy _____.

3. _____ have fun.

4. The dog _____.

Look at the picture. Read. Then draw
a line to make a complete sentence.

5. The kite  •   • are in the water.

6. Boats  •   • are made of sand.

7. The child  •   • flies in the sky.

8. Beaches  •   • picks up shells.

Describe

You can use words to **describe**. When you describe, you tell more about something. Read the words in the box. Then write a word to finish each sentence.

Describing Words

glad   sweet   long   hot

1. Becky feels _____glad_____.

2. The fire is _____.

3. The stick is _____.

4. Becky's apple is _____.

Read the words in the box.
Then write a word to finish each sentence.

Describing Words

funny   happy   hungry   quiet

5. The ____happy____ kids sit down.

6. Mike's _____ father eats.

7. The _____ movie starts.

8. The _____ children watch.

Write Sentences

Read the words in the box.
Choose words that begin with the same letter.
Make the words into a sentence. Write it on the line.

bees	smell	chirp	dig
dogs	chicks	buzz	skunks

1. <u>Bees buzz.</u>

2. _____

3. _____

4. _____

- -

Read the group of words. Make the words into a sentence.
Write the sentence on the line.

5. fish   The   swims

<u>The fish swims.</u>

6. eats   bird   A

_____

You can put sentences together. Sentences go in order from **first** to **last**. Look at the pictures. Read the words in the box. Then write a word from the box to finish each sentence.

The Sun Comes and Goes

First   Next   Last   Then

1. _____, the sun comes up in the morning.

2. _____, the sun is above us.

3. _____, the sun goes down at night.

4. _____, we see the stars and the moon.

Top Student • EMC 9321 • © Evan-Moor Corp.

Beginning, Middle, and End

Look at the pictures, and read the sentences.
They go together to make a story. Write **beginning**,
middle, or **end** to tell about each sentence.

1.

Amy opened
her yogurt.

_____

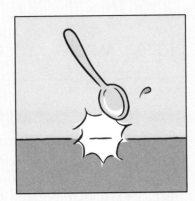

Amy's spoon fell
on the ground.

_____

Amy got a new
spoon and ate
her yogurt.

_____

Read the story. Write **beginning**, **middle**,
or **end** next to each sentence.

2. When Joe woke up, his head was sore. _____

3. Joe's mom felt his head with her hand. _____

4. Joe's mom said that Joe was sick. _____

Finish the Poems

Read the poem. On each line, write a word that rhymes with the color word. You can write words from the box or different words. The first one has been done for you.

float   face   oat   place   wrote   race   coat   goat   aunt

Little Ant

Oh, Little Ant,

I saw you on a ___plant___ .

I think I saw your uncle,

I think I saw your _____ .

What Is on the Boat?

I jump on the boat,

I hope it will _____ .

On the boat I see,

A square-shaped _____ .

The Race

We run, we rush, we chase,

There are many people at this _____ .

I have to tie my shoe,

I have to clean my _____ .

172

Give Reasons

Answer the question. Then draw. Last, write reasons.

1. What is your favorite animal?
   Write it. Then draw a picture of it.

   _____

2. Now write 3 reasons why this is your favorite animal.

   Reason 1: _____

   _____

   Reason 2: _____

   _____

   Reason 3: _____

   _____

3. What is your favorite food to eat for lunch?
   Write it. Then draw it on the plate.

   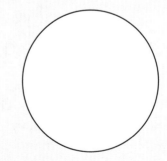

   _____

4. Now write 1 reason why this is your favorite lunch.

   Reason: _____

   _____

Tell What You Think

Read. Then answer the questions.

Suzi had a loose tooth. Her brother put a string around it. He pulled the string, and the tooth came out! Now Suzi cannot eat apples.

1. Did Suzi's brother help Suzi? Circle the answer.   **yes   no**

2. Why did you choose that answer? Write a sentence.

_____

_____

Read. Then answer the questions.

Have you ever seen a movie at the theater? Movies have different prices at different times. If you see a movie during the day, it will cost $5.00. If you see a movie at night, it will cost $7.00.

3. Is it better to see a movie during the day or at night? Circle the answer.   **day   night**

4. Why did you choose that answer? Write a sentence.

_____

_____

Write Something Make-Believe

Read. Then answer the questions.

A loud noise woke me up this morning. I looked out my window and saw a small squirrel carrying a big oak tree across the grass. "Hey!" I shouted, "Bring that back!" But the squirrel looked at me and kept on going.

1. This is about something _____.

   ○ real   ○ make-believe

   Tell how you know.

   _____

Read the sentence. Circle the sentence if it tells something make-believe.

2. A goat spoke to me in English.

3. I used my arms as wings and flew to the sun.

4. There is a hole in my sock.

Write a sentence that tells something make-believe.

5. _____

   _____

Tell More About the Topic

You can make a **paragraph**. A paragraph is a group of sentences. They tell about one topic. Read the bold sentence below that tells the topic.

Babies learn to do many things.

Now read the pair of sentences. Choose the sentence that tells more about the topic. Fill in the circle.

1. ○ Dogs love babies.   ○ Babies learn to crawl.

2. ○ Babies learn to stand.   ○ Babies don't have teeth at first.

3. ○ Babies learn to walk.   ○ Babies like to play.

4. ○ Babies make sounds.   ○ Babies learn to run.

- -

Which paragraph is made of the sentences above? Fill in the circle.

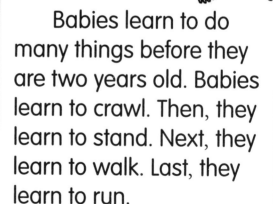

5.

Babies learn from seeing people around them. They learn how to eat solid food and drink from cups. They learn how to clap their hands. They learn other things, too.

Ⓐ

Babies learn to do many things before they are two years old. Babies learn to crawl. Then, they learn to stand. Next, they learn to walk. Last, they learn to run.

Ⓑ

Tell How Things Are the Same and Different

Think of the ways that a cat and a bird are the **same**. Think of the ways they are **different**. Then write 2 ways that cats and birds are the same and different.

SAME

1. _____

_____

2. _____

_____

DIFFERENT

1. _____

_____

2. _____

_____

Katie's Pencil

When you **suggest**, you tell an idea.
Read and follow the directions.

Katie's pencil broke. **Suggest** three ways Katie could solve her problem.

1. _____

2. _____

3. _____

Gabe's Problem

When you **solve**, you find an answer to a problem.
Gabe cannot find his book. Read and follow the directions.

Solve Gabe's problem. Write three things Gabe can do.

1. _____

2. _____

3. _____

What Happened?

Read the story Michael wrote about when he fell off his bike.

One day, I was riding bikes with my big brother. We both had on helmets. My brother was riding in front of me. Then a big dog ran in front of my brother's bike. My brother stopped fast! I tried to stop fast, too. But I could not slow down in time. My bike crashed into my brother's bike. I fell off my bike and hurt my leg. My brother helped me get home.

Now write a story about something that happened to you. You can write about a time you got hurt, like Michael. Or you can write about something else.

_____

_____

_____

_____

_____

My Thoughts

Draw a picture of your face.
Then write what you think in each thought cloud.

2. What is something you
can try to do better?

1. What is the
best thing
about you?

3. What do your
friends think
about you?

Mindful
Moments

track 1 🔊

Listen to the audio

For students in China

- Sit on the floor.

- Take the biggest breath you can through your nose.

- Breathe out as slowly as you can through your mouth.

- Take another deep breath. Take in as much air as you can.

- Pretend to blow out candles as you slowly breathe out.

182

Mindful Practice

- Now lie down on your back. Make sure your body feels comfy.

- Look around the room. Try to find as many shapes as you can.

- Listen. What do you hear? Can you hear yourself breathing?

- Feel. Think about what you feel right now. Can you feel your heartbeat?

Do you feel happy?

Do you feel sad?

Do you feel excited?

Do you feel sleepy?

184

Math

Jump, Frogs, Jump!

How far will each frog jump?
Use the number lines to help you.

1. This frog is going to make 2 more jumps.
On what number will it land? _____

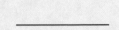
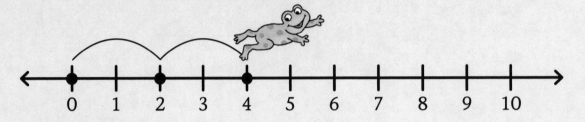

2. This frog is going to make 1 more jump.
On what number will it land? _____

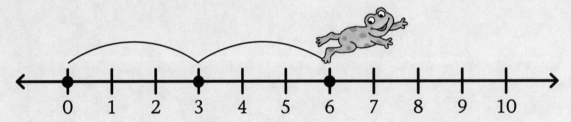

3. This frog is going to make 3 more jumps.
On what number will it land? _____

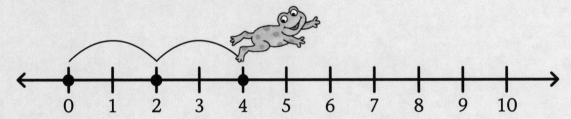

Snake Colors

Read about the snakes. Write the answers.

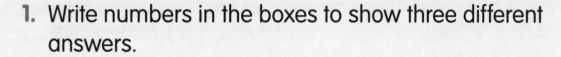

There are 9 snakes.
Some are green. Some are red.
There are more green snakes than red snakes.
How many green snakes and red snakes could there be?

1. Write numbers in the boxes to show three different answers.

  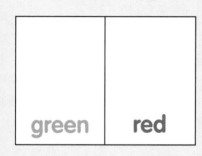

| green | red | | green | red | | green | red |

2. Color the snakes to show one of your answers.

Up the Mountain and Down Again

SKILL
Use addition and subtraction facts

Add your way up the mountain. Subtract your way down.
Draw a line between the facts with the same three numbers.

5 + 5 = ☐   10 − 5 = ☐

4 + 2 = ☐   6 − 2 = ☐

3 + 7 = ☐   10 − 7 = ☐

6 + 2 = ☐   8 − 2 = ☐

2 + 4 = ☐   6 − 4 = ☐

1 + 6 = ☐   7 − 6 = ☐

7 + 2 = ☐   9 − 2 = ☐

6 + 4 = ☐   10 − 4 = ☐

4 + 1 = ☐   5 − 1 = ☐

A House of Facts

Write the answers. Cut out the problems at the bottom.
Glue each in its fact family house.

3 + 6 = _____

9 − 6 = _____

glue

8 + 2 = _____

10 − 2 = _____

glue

4 + 3 = _____

7 − 3 = _____

glue

7 + 3 = _____

10 − 3 = _____

glue

| 6 + 3 = _____ | 3 + 4 = _____ | 2 + 8 = _____ | 3 + 7 = _____ |
| 9 − 3 = _____ | 7 − 4 = _____ | 10 − 8 = _____ | 10 − 7 = _____ |

Fruity Problems

Draw pictures to help you solve these problems.

1. Li picked 2 🍊 from one tree. She picked 3 🍊 from another tree. How many 🍊 did she pick?

   _____ oranges

2. There were 6 ◯ on a tree. Cara picked 3 of them. How many ◯ were still on the tree?

   _____ lemons

3. Azad had 2 🍐. Tara had 4 🍐. How many 🍐 did they have in all?

   _____ pears

4. Write a word problem about this picture.

_____

_____

_____

_____

_____

_____

Three Teddy Bears

Here are three teddy bears with bows. The bears are brown, yellow, and orange. The bows are blue, purple, and red. Read the clues. Then color the pictures to show which bow is on each bear.

Clues:

- The brown bear has the red bow or the purple bow.
- The yellow bear has the red bow or the blue bow.
- The orange bear does not have the red bow or the blue bow.

Be a Facts Detective!

See if you can spot the different ways to make the numbers below.

1. Circle ways to make **9**.

13 – 4	12 – 5
6 + 3	9 – 0
11 – 2	13 – 5
7 + 5	

2. Circle ways to make **10**.

4 + 9	12 – 2
3 + 7	13 – 3
11 – 1	6 + 4
10 – 5	

3. Circle ways to make **11**.

4 + 7

12 – 6

5 + 6

12 – 4

11 – 0

9 + 2

13 – 8

4. Circle ways to make **12**.

8 + 4

12 – 4

5 + 7

9 – 3

12 – 0

13 – 5

6 + 6

5. Circle ways to make **13**.

11 + 2

12 – 9

6 + 7

10 + 3

11 – 5

4 + 9

13 – 0

A Flock of Birds

Write a number sentence to solve each problem.

1. There are 6 birds on the ground. Then 7 more birds come.
How many birds are there now?

_____ ⬤ _____ = _____   _____ birds

2. There are 8 black birds and 4 green birds in a tree.
How many more black birds than green birds are there?

_____ ⬤ _____ = _____   _____ more

3. Write a word problem about this picture.
Then write the number sentence about it.

_____

_____

_____ ⬤ _____ = _____

194

Rows of Patterns

Circle the repeating unit. Then use the letters **A**, **B**, and **C** to write the pattern.

1.   A   B   A   B   A   B   A   B

2.   ___ ___ ___ ___ ___ ___ ___ ___ ___

3.   ___ ___ ___ ___ ___ ___ ___ ___ ___

4.   ___ ___ ___ ___ ___ ___ ___ ___

5.   ___ ___ ___ ___ ___ ___ ___ ___ ___

Draw an **ABC** pattern here.

6.

___ ___ ___ ___ ___ ___ ___ ___

Buzz, Buzz!

Count the bees. Then write how many bees are inside the hive.

1. There are 12 bees in all.

_____ bees are in the hive.

2. There are 14 bees in all.

_____ bees are in the hive.

3. There are 13 bees in all.

_____ bees are in the hive.

4. There are 15 bees in all.

_____ bees are in the hive.

5. There are 17 bees in all.

_____ bees are in the hive.

6. There are 16 bees in all.

_____ bees are in the hive.

Corner Cutouts

Jesse had four paper rectangles.
He cut one corner off each rectangle.
Circle the shapes that he cut out.
(Some shapes have been turned around.)

1.

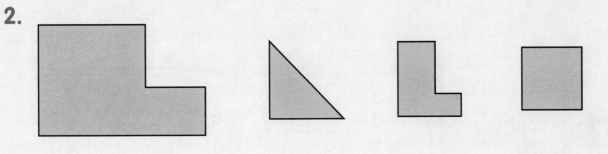

2.

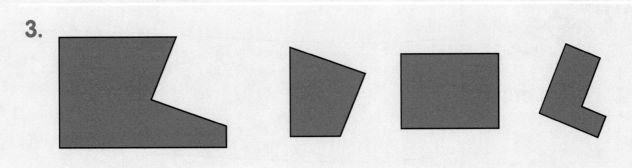

3.

4.

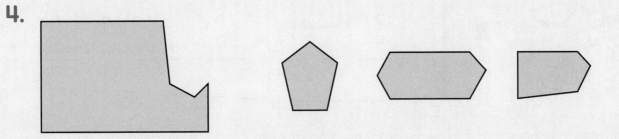

High-Flying Banners

Look at each set of numbers.
Add the two numbers that make **10**.
Then add the last number.

★ **Tip:** When you add three numbers, sometimes you can make **10** first. This helps you add more easily.

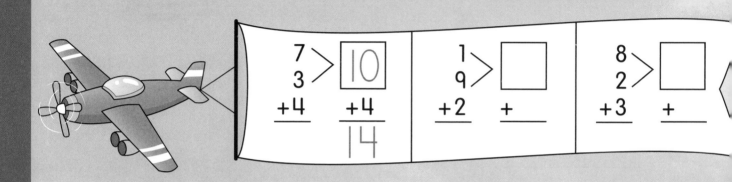

$$
\begin{array}{r} 7 \\ 3 \\ +4 \end{array} \rangle \boxed{10} \quad \begin{array}{r} +4 \\ \hline 14 \end{array}
$$

$$
\begin{array}{r} 1 \\ 9 \\ +2 \end{array} \rangle \Box \quad +
$$

$$
\begin{array}{r} 8 \\ 2 \\ +3 \end{array} \rangle \Box \quad +
$$

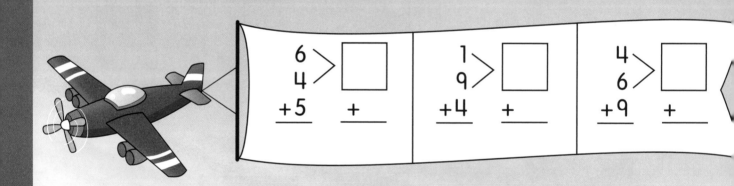

$$
\begin{array}{r} 6 \\ 4 \\ +5 \end{array} \rangle \Box \quad +
$$

$$
\begin{array}{r} 1 \\ 9 \\ +4 \end{array} \rangle \Box \quad +
$$

$$
\begin{array}{r} 4 \\ 6 \\ +9 \end{array} \rangle \Box \quad +
$$

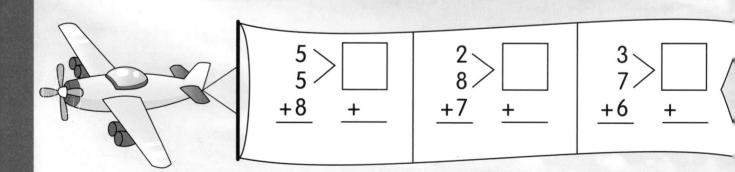

$$
\begin{array}{r} 5 \\ 5 \\ +8 \end{array} \rangle \Box \quad +
$$

$$
\begin{array}{r} 2 \\ 8 \\ +7 \end{array} \rangle \Box \quad +
$$

$$
\begin{array}{r} 3 \\ 7 \\ +6 \end{array} \rangle \Box \quad +
$$

In the Woods

SKILLS
Solve word problems: Add three numbers;
Write number sentences

Read and solve the problems.

1. 3 campers went fishing. 5 campers went swimming. 4 campers went hiking. How many campers were there in all?

   _____ campers

2. Tony saw some birds. He saw 7 jays and 3 hawks. Then he saw 4 quails. How many birds did he see in all?

   _____ birds

3. Kim, Candy, and Maria went fishing. Each girl caught 5 fish. How many fish did they catch in all?

   _____ fish

4. Write a word problem about this picture. Then write a number sentence about it.

   _____

   _____

   _____

   _____

   ____ ◯ ____ ◯ ____ = ____

Bowls of Cherries

Fill in the missing numbers to show the number of cherries.

 = 1 ten    = 1 one

1.    <u> 2 </u> <u> 3 </u> <u> 23 </u>
                                            tens   ones   in all

2.    <u>   </u> <u>   </u> <u>   </u>
                                            tens   ones   in all

3.   <u>   </u> <u>   </u> <u>   </u>
                                            tens   ones   in all

4.   <u>   </u> <u>   </u> <u>   </u>
                                            tens   ones   in all

5.   <u>   </u> <u>   </u> <u>   </u>
                                            tens   ones   in all

6.   <u>   </u> <u>   </u> <u>   </u>
                                            tens   ones   in all

Write in your own numbers to complete the table.

Tens	Ones	In All

Balloons for Sale

13 is **less than** 50	80 is **greater than** 50
13 $<$ 50	80 $>$ 50

Color the balloons.

Use  for numbers **less than** 50.

Use (purple) for numbers **greater than** 50.

Write **<** or **>**.

19 $<$ 50   83 ◯ 50   51 ◯ 50   27 ◯ 50

64 ◯ 50   15 ◯ 50   49 ◯ 50   65 ◯ 50

Find the Numbers

Use the hundred chart to write the missing numbers.

1	2	3	4	5	6	7	8	9	10
11	12	13	14	15	16	17	18	19	20
21	22	23	24	25	26	27	28	29	30
31	32	33	34	35	36	37	38	39	40
41	42	43	44	45	46	47	48	49	50
51	52	53	54	55	56	57	58	59	60
61	62	63	64	65	66	67	68	69	70
71	72	73	74	75	76	77	78	79	80
81	82	83	84	85	86	87	88	89	90
91	92	93	94	95	96	97	98	99	100

one more	one less	ten more	ten less
6 ___7___	___2___ 3	6 ___16___	___7___ 17
11 _____	_____ 21	12 _____	_____ 29
20 _____	_____ 12	19 _____	_____ 56
36 _____	_____ 35	37 _____	_____ 82
10 _____	_____ 70	7 _____	_____ 40
42 _____	_____ 86	30 _____	_____ 35
24 _____	_____ 67	46 _____	_____ 91
49 _____	_____ 100	14 _____	_____ 77

Hiking Back

Help the hikers get back to their tents. Count backward from **100** to **70**. Write the numbers on the path.

100

94

85

78

70

Mama Elephants

There are three elephant mothers in a family.
Their ages are **37**, **15**, and **27**. Write their ages
in order from the youngest to the oldest.

_____   _____   _____

1. Is the middle elephant closer in age
   to the oldest or the youngest?   _____

2. How many years older is the oldest
   elephant than the middle elephant?   _____ years older

3. How many years older is the middle
   elephant than the youngest elephant?   _____ years older

Favorite Pets

Look at the graph to answer the questions.

Our Favorite Pets							
dog	🐕	🐕	🐕	🐕	🐕	🐕	🐕
cat	🐈	🐈	🐈				
mouse	🐁	🐁					
bird	🐦	🐦	🐦				
hamster	🐹	🐹	🐹	🐹	🐹		
snake	🐍						
	1	2	3	4	5	6	7

Animals

1. Which pet is the most favorite? _____

2. Which pet is the least favorite? _____

3. Which **two** pets were picked by the same number of children?

   _____ and _____

4. Write something else you learned from the graph.

   _____

   _____

Getting to School

Look at the bar graph. Answer the questions.

How do you go to school?					
car					
bike					
walk					
	1	2	3	4	5

1. What is this bar graph about? _____

   _____

2. How many more children walk than ride a bike?

   _____ more children

3. How do most children go to school?
   ○ car   bike   ○ walk

4. How many children answered the question? _____ children

Top Student • EMC 9321 • © Evan-Moor Corp.

Where Is the Bear Sleeping?

Count by **tens** to **100**.

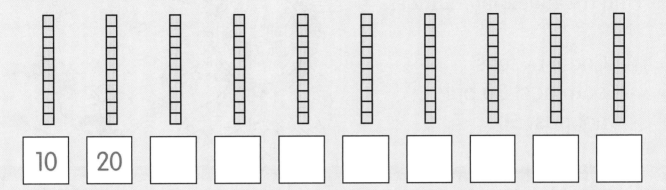

| 10 | 20 | | | | | | | | |

Count by **tens**. Connect the dots from **10** to **100** in order.

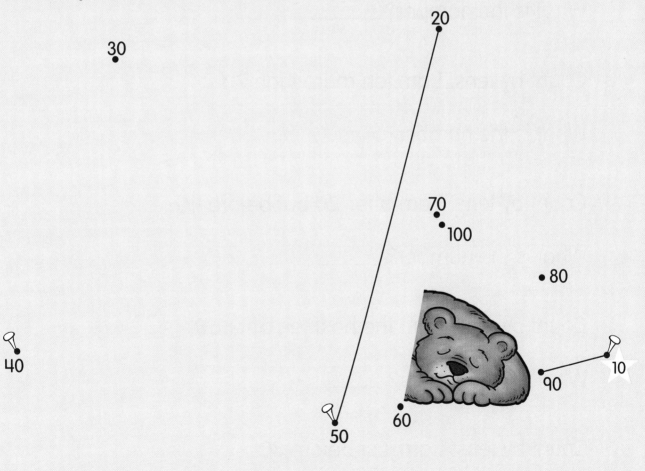

What Is the Number?

Read the clues.
Find the matching number.

1. Count by tens.
    I am past **30** but
    not past **50**.

    What is the number? _____

2. Count by tens. I am between **80** and **100**.

    What is the number? _____

3. Count by tens. I am ten more than **70**.

    What is the number? _____

4. Count by tens. I am after **20** but before **40**.

    What is the number? _____

5. Count by tens. I am the next ten after **50**.

    What is the number? _____

6. Count by tens. I am just before **80**.

    What is the number? _____

Counting Patterns

Skip-count.

1. Count by **tens**. Color each number you counted **yellow**.

2. Count by **fives**. Draw a circle around each number you counted.

3. Count by **twos**. Draw an **X** on each number you counted.

1	☒ 2	3	☒ 4	⑤	6	7	8	9	⑩
11	12	13	14	15	16	17	18	19	20
21	22	23	24	25	26	27	28	29	30
31	32	33	34	35	36	37	38	39	40
41	42	43	44	45	46	47	48	49	50
51	52	53	54	55	56	57	58	59	60
61	62	63	64	65	66	67	68	69	70
71	72	73	74	75	76	77	78	79	80
81	82	83	84	85	86	87	88	89	90
91	92	93	94	95	96	97	98	99	100

4. Describe the numbers that were colored yellow, circled, AND covered by an **X**.

_____

Barnyard Riddles

Use the code to answer the riddles.
Write the matching letter below
each sum.

Use the code to answer the riddles.

26–**a**	38–**o**	53–**t**
27–**e**	48–**r**	65–**u**
34–**k**	49–**s**	98–**y**

What do you call a farmer's alarm clock?

13 +13	36 +12	30 + 8	18 +20	15 +34	22 +31	11 +16	25 +23
26							
a							

What kind of key will you find in a barnyard?

15 +11	21 +32	23 +42	31 +17	14 +20	14 +13	61 +37

Rescue the King

Help the knight reach the king and rescue him.
Color the boxes with the answer **35 orange**.

49 −14 **35**	80 −10	77 −65	59 −27	65 −54
46 −11	75 −40	68 −33	99 −10	29 −16
86 −32	99 −46	59 −24	47 −14	58 −27
78 −44	55 −35	98 −63		

Porcupine Stories

Read the problems and solve them.
Write number sentences to help you solve the problems.

1. Spike and Prickles are porcupines. Spike weighs 15 pounds. Prickles weighs 12 pounds. How much do they weigh together?

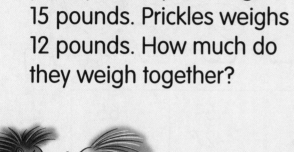

_____ pounds

2. A porcupine ate 10 green leaves, 10 yellow leaves, and 6 brown leaves. How many leaves did it eat?

_____ leaves

3. Sharpy's head and body together are 30 inches long. Sharpy's tail is 8 inches long. How long is Sharpy from head to tail?

_____ inches

4. There were 3 porcupine families. Each family had 6 members. How many porcupines were there in all?

_____ porcupines

Pick a Lunch

Mr. Garcia is taking a lunch count at school. Color the boxes to show how many of each item he counted.

hamburger	ⵜⵜⵜ ⵜⵜⵜ ⵜⵜⵜ III
sandwich	III
pizza	ⵜⵜⵜ II
taco	ⵜⵜⵜ
milk	ⵜⵜⵜ ⵜⵜⵜ ⵜⵜⵜ
juice	ⵜⵜⵜ III

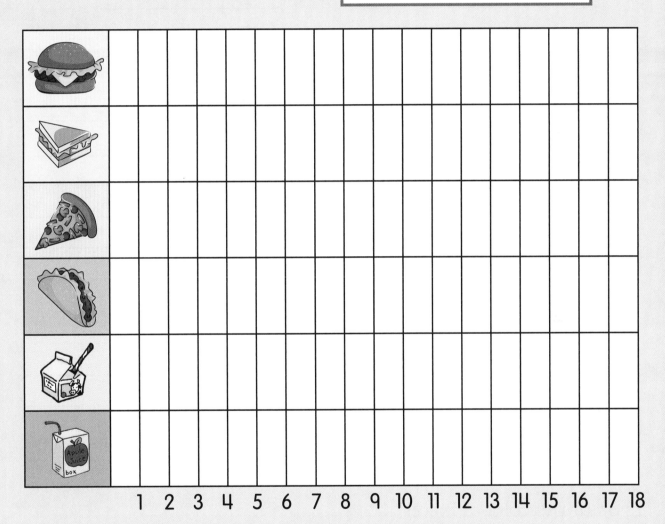

1 2 3 4 5 6 7 8 9 10 11 12 13 14 15 16 17 18

Write two things this graph shows you.

1. _____

2. _____

Name Game

Write the names of 3 friends.
Count the number of letters in their names.

__George__ __6__ _____ ____

_____ ____ _____ ____

Write the names below the graph.
Color a box for each letter in each name.

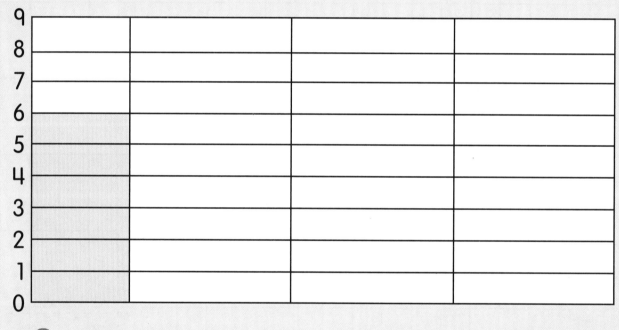

George _____ _____ _____

Look at the colored boxes.

1. Who has the longest name? _____

2. Write two more things this graph shows you. _____

_____

The Same Amount

Show each amount of money two ways.
Cut out the coins. Glue them in the boxes.

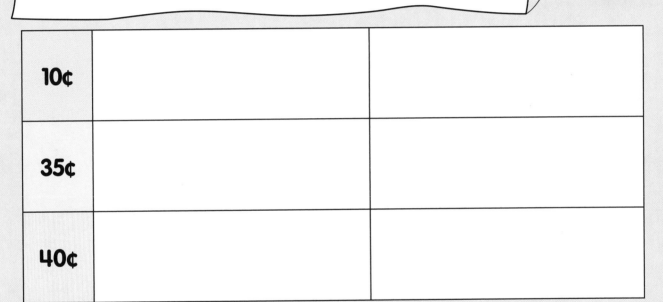

10¢		
35¢		
40¢		

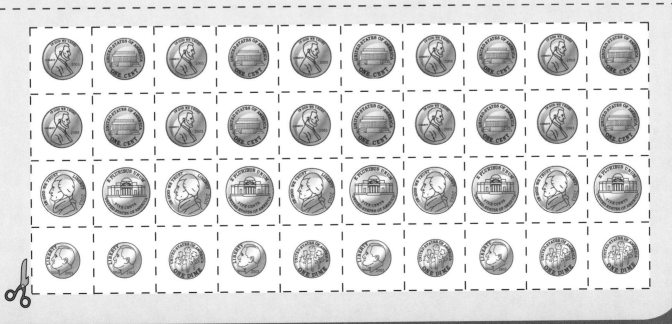

Eraser Fun

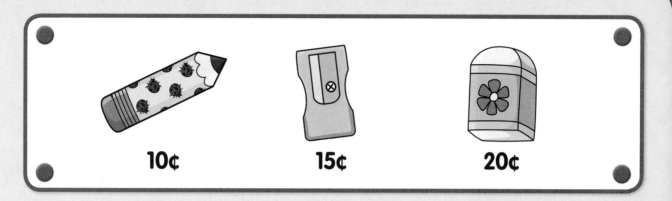

10¢   15¢   20¢

Circle the coins you need. Then write the amounts.

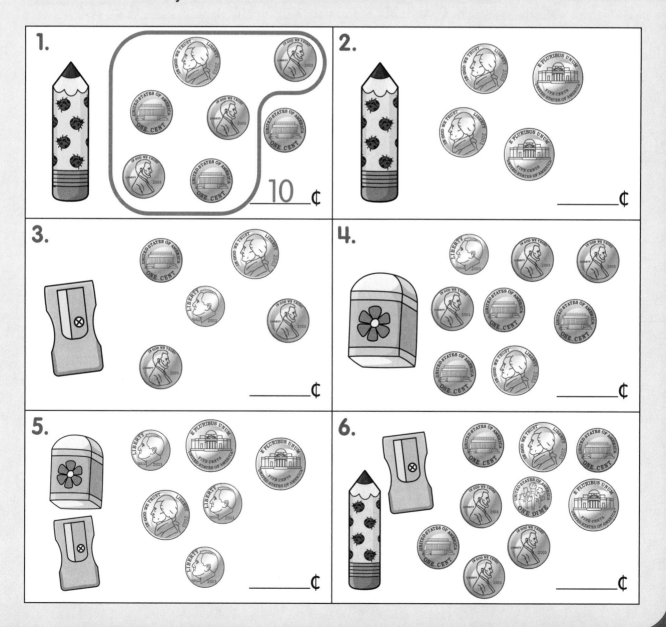

1. 10 ¢

2. _____ ¢

3. _____ ¢

4. _____ ¢

5. _____ ¢

6. _____ ¢

What Is Missing?

Look at how much you have. Look at how much you need.
Write and draw the missing amount.

1.

8¢ + _____¢ = 10¢

2.

9¢ + _____¢ = 16¢

3.

8¢ + _____¢ = 14¢

4.

9¢ + _____¢ = 12¢

Fill in the missing amount.

5. 8¢ + _____¢ = 13¢

6. 5¢ + _____¢ = 15¢

7. 10¢ + _____¢ = 20¢

8. 8¢ + _____¢ = 16¢

9. 9¢ + _____¢ = 13¢

10. 4¢ + _____¢ = 11¢

11. 7¢ + _____¢ = 14¢

12. 5¢ + _____¢ = 10¢

Wild Animal Park

Read the problems and solve them.

1. Theo is at a wild animal park. He buys treats to feed the giraffes. The treats cost 70¢. He pays with 5 dimes and some nickels. How many nickels does Theo use?

_____ nickels

2. Maria wants to buy a tiger poster. It costs 85¢. She has 2 quarters. How much more money does she need?

_____¢ more

3. Cory buys 3 postcards of pandas. Each postcard costs 20¢. How much money does he pay?

_____¢

What Time Is It?

Look at the time on the analog clock. Write the time on the digital clock.

★ **Example:**

1.

2.

3.

4.

5.

6.

My Day

Write the time you do each thing.
Draw hands on the clocks to match.

1. I get up. _____		
2. I start school. _____		
3. I eat lunch. _____		
4. I eat dinner. _____		
5. I go to bed. _____		

Pattern Challenge

1. Color the balloons to show a pattern.
   The pattern must have 3 yellow and 6 red balloons.

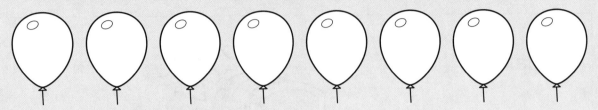

2. Color the bears to show a pattern.
   Use three colors.

3. Color the flowers to show a pattern.
   Use three colors. Flowers 1 and 5 must be the same color.

4. Draw a pattern using a ◯ and a ☐.
   The pattern must be different from the others.

Seals at Sea

Read the problems and solve them.

1. Three seals were eating. Each seal ate 4 fish and 5 shrimp. How many fish and shrimp were eaten in all?

_____ fish and

_____ shrimp

2. A harbor seal ate 10 pounds of food. A gray seal ate 35 pounds of food. How much more did the gray seal eat than the harbor seal?

_____ more pounds

3. There were 67 seals on the rocks. Soon, 20 jumped into the water. Then 30 more jumped in. How many seals were still on the rocks?

_____ seals

4. A seal went into the ocean. It swam for 33 minutes. It ate for 18 minutes. It took a nap for 47 minutes. Then it came back to the beach. How many minutes was the seal in the ocean?

_____ minutes

Four Friendly Visitors

SKILL
Use logical thinking

Read the clues to find out the name of each alien visitor.
Then write the names above their pictures.

Clues: Ig is taller than Ork.

Zep is taller than Bax.

Ork is taller than Zep.

Top Student • EMC 9321 • © Evan-Moor Corp.

Let's Measure

Look at the cubes to measure each item.
Write the length.

1.

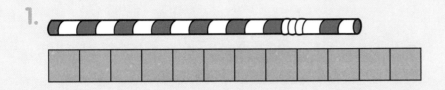

_____ squares

2.

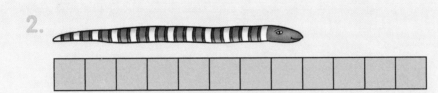

_____ squares

3.

_____ squares

4.

_____ squares

5. Draw your own picture and measure it.

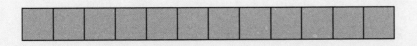

_____ squares

Measure and Compare

Measure. Write a number sentence to help you compare.

1.

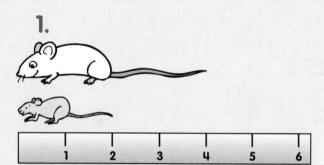

$$\underline{\quad 4 \quad} \;\bigcirc\!\!-\!\! \;\underline{\quad 2 \quad} = \underline{\quad 2 \quad}$$

The white mouse is

___2___ inches longer.

2.

$$\underline{\qquad} \;\bigcirc\; \underline{\qquad} = \underline{\qquad}$$

The worm is

_____ centimeters longer.

3.

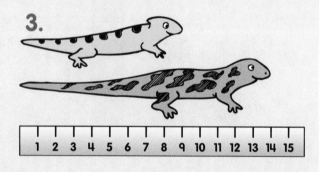

$$\underline{\qquad} \;\bigcirc\; \underline{\qquad} = \underline{\qquad}$$

The green lizard is

_____ centimeters longer.

4.

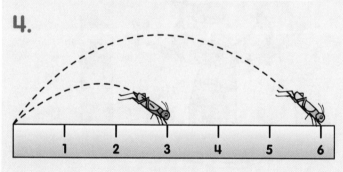

$$\underline{\qquad} \;\bigcirc\; \underline{\qquad} = \underline{\qquad}$$

The green cricket jumped

_____ inches farther.

Fun with Patterns

SKILLS
Analyze, extend, and create patterns;
Use spatial reasoning

Connect the dots to continue each pattern.

1.

2.
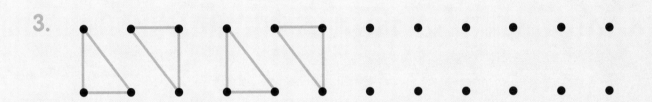

3.
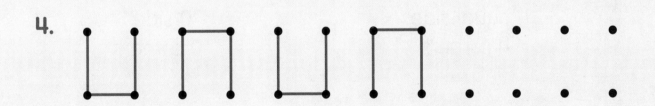

4.

5. Connect the dots to make your own pattern.

I Can Draw Shapes

Read how many sides and corners. Draw the shape.

1.

4 sides
4 corners

2.

3 sides
3 corners

3.

4 equal sides
4 corners

4.

0 sides
0 corners

5. How are a ⬜ and a ▭ alike?

_____

6. How are a ⬜ and a ▭ different?

_____

Make Bigger Shapes

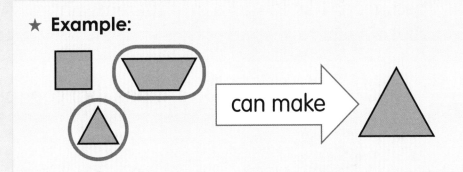

★ **Example:**

can make

Circle the smaller shapes that can be used
to make the bigger shape.

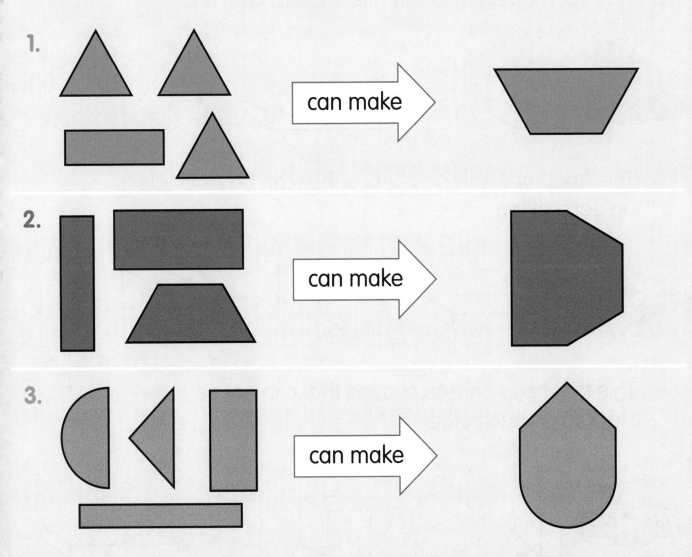

1.

can make

2.

can make

3.

can make

Jump, Frogs, Jump!

These frogs like to jump on different shapes.
Color the shapes.

1. This frog hops only on shapes that can roll.

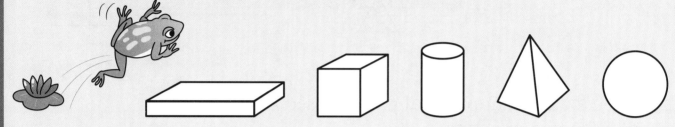

2. This frog hops only on shapes that can <u>not</u> roll.

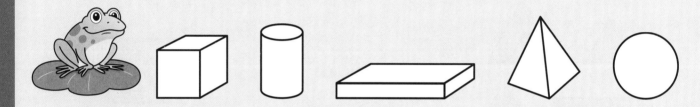

3. This frog hops only on shapes that can be stacked on each other.

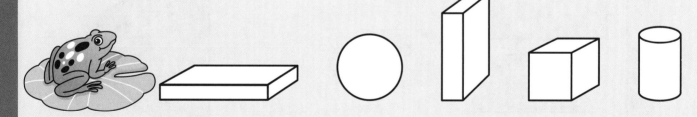

4. This frog hops only on shapes that can <u>not</u> be stacked on each other.

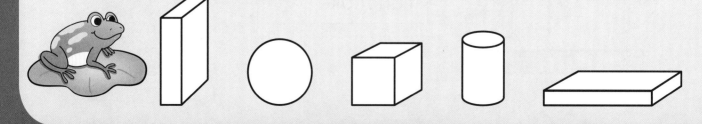

Fun with Blocks

Draw a line from each group of shapes to the new shape you can make.

1.   •   •

2.   •   •

3. 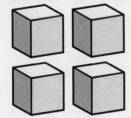 •   •

4. 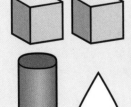 •   •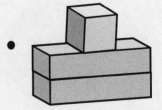

5. 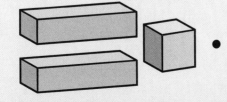 •   •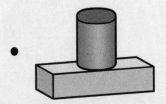

Tasty Foods

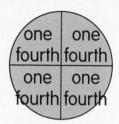

★ **Halves** are two equal shares of a whole.

★ **Thirds** are three equal shares of a whole.

★ **Fourths** are four equal shares of a whole.

Circle the foods.

1. Circle each food that shows **one half** shaded.

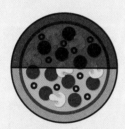
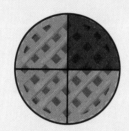

2. Circle each food that shows **one third** shaded.

3. Circle each food that shows **one fourth** shaded.

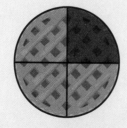

Top Student • EMC 9321 • © Evan-Moor Corp.

Sharing Lunch

Draw lines to make equal shares.

1. Keisha gave one half of her sandwich to Leo. Draw a line to make equal shares. Make an **X** on the part Keisha gave Leo.

2. Sara gave one third of her cheese to Ian. Draw lines to make equal shares. Make an **X** on the part Sara gave Ian.

3. Yoko gave one half of her orange to Nico. Draw a line to make equal shares. Make an **X** on the part that Yoko gave Nico.

4. Karl gave one fourth of his cookie to Jamal. Draw lines to make equal shares. Make an **X** on the part Karl gave Jamal.

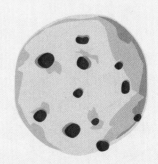

What's the Side View?

Circle the drawing that shows what each stack of blocks looks like from the shaded side.

1.

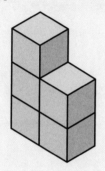 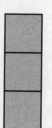 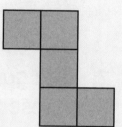

2.

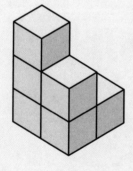 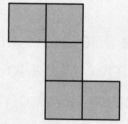 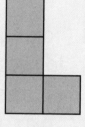

3.

 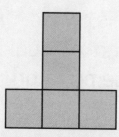 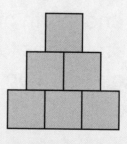 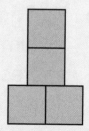

A Shell Collection

Shawn collects shells. He keeps them in square boxes and round boxes. All the square boxes have the same number of shells. All the round boxes have the same number of shells. Look at the pictures. Find out how many shells are in each box.

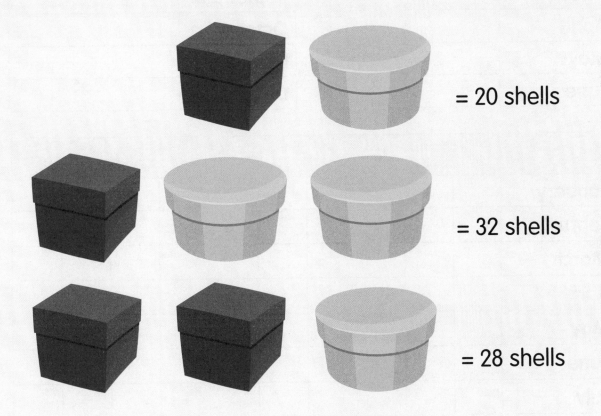

= 20 shells

= 32 shells

= 28 shells

1. How many shells are in one square box? _____

2. How many shells are in one round box? _____

When Were You Born?

Ask ten people you know what month they were born in. You can ask your family and friends. Use the tally sheet to mark each answer. Then make a bar graph to how show many.

Months	Tally Marks
January	
February	
March	
April	
May	
June	

Months	Tally Marks
July	
August	
September	
October	
November	
December	

Birthday Months

January										
February										
March										
April										
May										
June										
July										
August										
September										
October										
November										
December										

1 2 3 4 5 6 7 8 9 10

Sweet Shopping

Read the story and the question. Think about what you would like best. Answer the questions.

Your aunt gave you $1. She takes you to a candy store. You see these candies for sale.

$1 each

20¢ each

Would you buy one big candy bar or 5 small pieces?

_____

Explain your choice.

_____

_____

_____

Split a Shape

Split a shape to make new shapes.
Then glue them back together to make
an interesting design!

What You Need

- colored paper
- white paper
- glue

What You Do

1. Cut out a shape from colored paper.

2. Draw one or two lines to split the shape.
   Make the lines straight, jagged, or curved.
   Cut on the lines.

3. Put the shape back together on white paper,
   but leave a little space between the parts.
   Glue the pieces onto the white paper.
   Look at your new design!

4. Make more designs with split shapes.
   Here are some ideas:

   - Use the same shape but change where the line goes.
   - Use different shapes but keep the lines the same.
   - For one shape, draw two lines that are close together.
     For another shape, draw two lines that are far apart.

Computer Science

How Computers Work

Read. Then answer the items.

Do you like to play games on computers or phones? These games are made with **code**. A code is a group of letters, numbers, and other signs. A person writes a code. A code tells the computer game what to do. A code tells steps, or directions. Computers follow the steps. That's how computers and computer games work.

Computer turn off # ! ☺

Computers do jobs. When you turn on a computer, the computer does the job of turning on. What happens when you press a letter? You see the letter on the screen. This means the computer is working. People can do jobs like computers do. We can follow steps. We can make a bigger job into some smaller jobs. Each small job helps you do the bigger job. Think about

a job you can do, like writing your name. Writing your name is the bigger job. Writing each letter is a smaller job. After you write all the letters, you finish the bigger job. Computers can also make bigger jobs into smaller jobs.

Top Student • EMC 9321 • © Evan-Moor Corp.

Computers work because of coding and patterns. Do you like to find patterns? If you do, then you might be good at coding. When a computer doesn't work, it might be because there is a mistake in the coding. The people who write code are called **coders**. It is important for coders to follow and write steps correctly. Then our computers work!

A B C A B C A B C A B C A B C

Answer the items.

1. Will a computer work if there is a mistake in the code? Tell why.

_____

_____

2. Write what will happen if a code tells a computer to make a sound every time you turn on the computer.

_____

_____

How Computers Work

Cut out the pictures. Then glue them in order to tell how to make a cake. The first one has been done for you.

> An **algorithm** is a list of **steps** you need to follow to complete a task. The steps below are part of an algorithm.

Put on the frosting and eat it up.

Stir up the cake mix.

Put it in the pan and bake it.

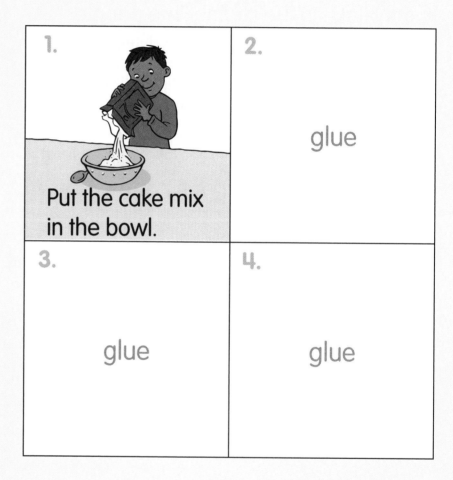

1. Put the cake mix in the bowl.

2. glue

3. glue

4. glue

Follow the Steps

A computer follows **steps**, just like people do.
Read the steps. Then do what each step says.

Step 1: Trace the square.

Step 2: Color the square.

Step 3: Draw one more square.

Read the steps. Then do what each step says.

Step 1: Draw a face in the circle.

Step 2: Draw ears on the outside of the circle.

Step 3: Draw hair on the circle.

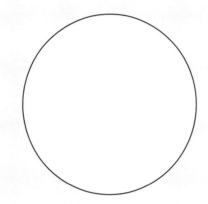

Read the steps. Then do what each step says.

Step 1: Write how many years old you are on the line.

_____ years old

Step 2: Draw the same number of triangles as your age.

Matching Patterns

Coders write steps. They also find **patterns**, or things that repeat. You can practice what coders do.

Color to make squares 1 and 2 match.

1.

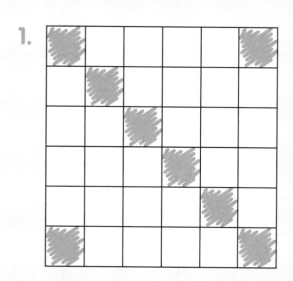

2.

Color to make squares 3 and 4 match.

3.

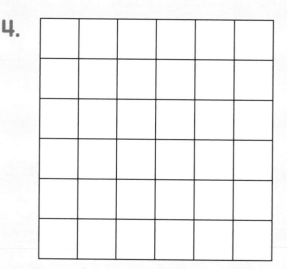

4.

Patterns and Steps

Look at the colored squares. Read the words.
Then match the square to the words that tell the steps.

1. 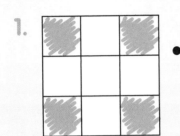 •   •

Step 1: Get a red marker.

Step 2: Color the top right corner square.

2. 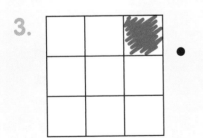 •   •

Step 1: Get a green marker.

Step 2: Color the bottom row.

Step 3: Color the center square.

3.  •   •

Step 1: Get a green marker.

Step 2: Color the top right corner square.

Step 3: Color the top left corner square.

Step 4: Color the bottom right corner square.

Step 5: Color the bottom left corner square.

Help Ava Find Flowers

SKILLS
Use visual discrimination; Relate text to
pictures; Write steps

Ava wants to pick flowers, but she has to find them.
The blue arrows show the way. Each blue arrow is
a **step**. Write the words from the box to tell the steps
Ava should follow.

go right   go down   go up   go left

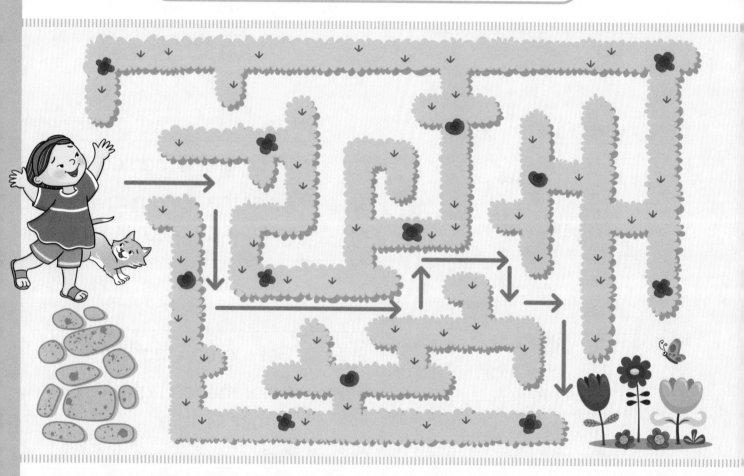

Step 1: _____   Step 5: _____

Step 2: _____   Step 6: _____

Step 3: _____   Step 7: _____

Step 4: _____   Step 8: _____

Which Button?

There are red and green buttons. You are pressing the buttons in a pattern. Find the pattern. On the line, write **red** or **green** to tell which button comes next.

1. 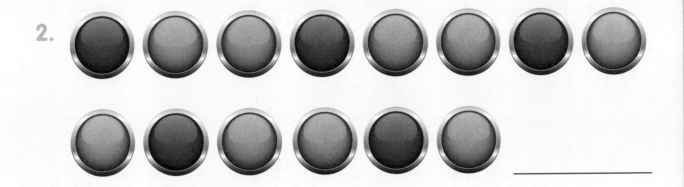 _____

2. 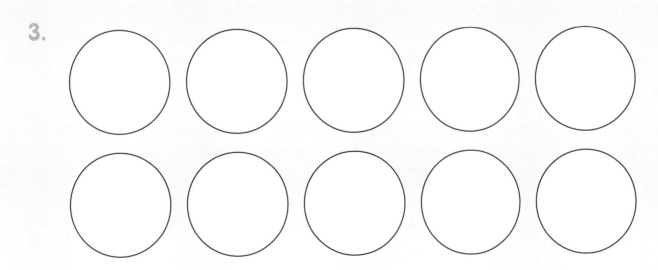 _____

Color the buttons to make a pattern. Use any colors you want.

3.

Find the Pattern

Look at the pictures. Can you find the pattern?
Answer the question below.

1.
  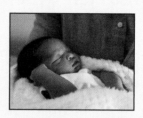 

  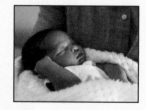 

What should come next in the pattern?
Fill in the circle below the picture.

  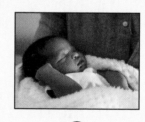 

Look at the shapes. Can you find the pattern?
Answer the question below.

2. ▲ ▲ ● ● ■ ■ ★ [?]

Write the color and shape that comes next in the pattern.

_____ _____
        color   shape

Write Patterns

People who write codes for computers use **patterns**. You can practice writing patterns. Look at the patterns below. Draw or write in the boxes to finish the patterns.

1.

X   A   X   B   X   C   X   D   X   ☐

X   F   X   G   X   ☐   X   I   ☐

2.

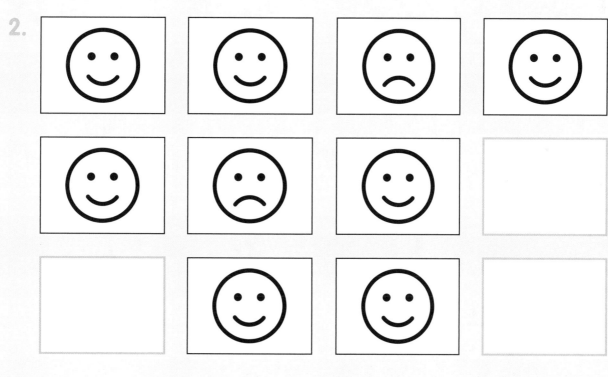

3.

1   A   2   B   3   C   4   D

5   E   6   F   7   ☐   8   H   ☐   I

Find the Bug in the Pattern

In a pattern, a **bug** is a mistake. Coders try to find bugs. Find the bug in each pattern below. Circle it.

1.

2.

3.

A   B   1   C   D   2   E   F

3   G   H   4   I   J   K   5

Use a Code

The letters and numbers show a **code**. The numbers stand for letters. You will use numbers to write words.

A=1	G=7	M=3	S=19	Y=25
B=2	H=8	N=14	T=20	Z=26
C=3	I=9	O=15	U=21	
D=4	J=10	P=16	V=22	
E=5	K=11	Q=17	W=23	
F=6	L=12	R=18	X=24	

1. Use numbers to write your first name.
   Write as many numbers as you need to.

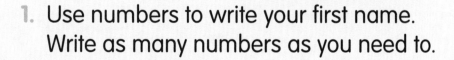

2. Write a word that tells about you. Use numbers.
   Space the numbers out on the line.

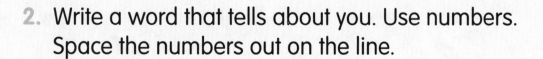

© Evan-Moor Corp. • EMC 9321 • Top Student   **251**

Feelings and Coding

SKILLS
Social and Emotional Learning:
Use inference skills; Connect facial
expressions to feelings

Have you ever seen an **emoji** like this one?
People use them on phones and computers.
Emojis are small pictures. Coders made them.
There is an emoji language! There are many
different kinds of emojis. People use them to
show feelings and thoughts.

Look at each emoji below. What do you
think it means? Write how you could use it.
Use a word from the box.

> silly   surprised   mad   sad

1. I could use this emoji to show that I feel _____.

2. I could use this emoji to show that I feel _____.

3. I could use this emoji to show that I feel _____.

4. I could use this emoji to show that I think

something is _____.

Science

What Is Vibration?

Read. Then answer the items.

Something that **vibrates** moves quickly back and forth. This movement is called **vibration**. We can feel vibration. We can also hear vibration. When an object vibrates, it makes the area around it vibrate, too. If something vibrates in water, then the water vibrates. If something vibrates in air, then the air vibrates. This is how you can feel something vibrate even if you are not touching it.

A vibration makes waves of sound in the air. The sound waves move through the air and into our ears. When the waves go inside our ears, our eardrums vibrate. Then the eardrum passes the vibrations through three little bones in the ear. The vibrations go through the inner ear. Last, the vibrations go into the brain. When the waves reach the brain, we know we have heard a sound. This all happens very quickly!

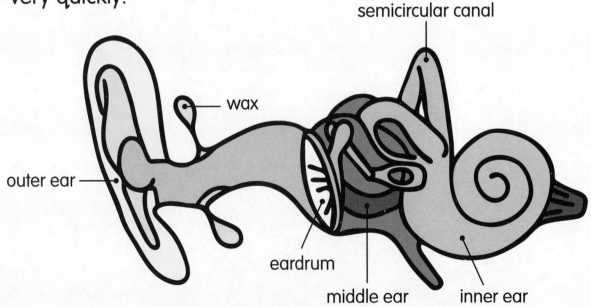

semicircular canal

wax

outer ear

eardrum

middle ear

inner ear

SKILL
Demonstrate understanding that vibrations
make sound waves that create sound

Answer the items.

1. What is vibration?

   _____

   _____

2. How can you feel an object's vibration even if you are
   not touching it?

   ○ You can feel the air vibrating.

   ○ You do not feel things when you touch them.

   ○ Your body vibrates when objects far away do.

3. What are sound waves?

   _____

   _____

4. How does an eardrum help you hear?

   _____

   _____

Seeing Sound Vibrations

You will do an experiment. You will see vibrations that make sound. In the experiment, the balloon will act like an eardrum. You just read about how eardrums pass sound vibrations to the inner ear.

What You Do

1. Cut a balloon and stretch it across the top of the open coffee can. Secure it with a rubber band.

2. Place a teaspoon of sugar in the center of the balloon.

3. Hold a metal pan close to the can and bang on the pan with a spoon.

4. Observe what happens.

5. Then do the activity on page 257.

What You Need

- balloon
- coffee can with both ends removed
- large rubber band
- sugar
- metal pan
- metal spoon
- page 257

Cut and glue in the correct order to tell what happened.

Seeing Sound

1.

glue

2.

glue

3.

glue

4.

glue

5.

glue

Sound waves traveled through the air and hit the balloon.

The balloon vibrated.

The sugar moved.

The sugar was still.

The spoon hit the pan and made sound waves.

Can Light Shine Through?

Answer the question for each picture.

Can the light shine through?
Circle **yes** or **no**.

window	yes no
apple	yes no
rubber duck	yes no
glass of water	yes no
book	yes no

How Do We See?

You use your eyes to see. But you also see because of light! If there is no light, you cannot see anything. Follow the steps below to see why light is important. Think about the questions as you do the experiments.

Reading Experiment

What You Need

- a room or closet that you can make very dark inside
- a book or paper with words to read

What You Do

1. Make the room as dark as you can. Then try to read. Can you see the words?

2. Let a little bit of light into the room. Then try to read. Can you see the words better?

3. Make the room as bright as you can. Then try to read. Can you read more easily?

From Far Away

SKILLS
Apply knowledge of scientific concepts to
answer questions; Write to explain

You can hear a sound when you are very close to what is
making the sound. But what if you are far away? Read the
list of sounds. Circle the ones that you could hear even if
you were across the street from what was making the sound.

1. thunder   a police siren   a sniff   a breath

Imagine that you can see a person who is far away. The person
cannot see or hear you. What tools could you use to make the
person see or hear you? Circle the tools you could use.

2. a flashlight   a pencil   a whistle   a book

Read the paragraph. Then answer the question.

A long time ago, people used smoke and fire to talk
to people who were far away. The fire made a bright light.
People could see it. When the fire was covered, it made
smoke. The people made patterns with the smoke. The
patterns stood for words. Today, people use smoke torches
to make colorful smoke that can be seen from far away.
People also used drums to let others hear them from far
away. Native Americans could make sound patterns
by beating the drums. Many people used horns, too.

3. How do sound and light help people talk to others
who are far away?

_____

_____

Scientists Group Things

When you **group** things, you put them together because they are the same in some way. Decide which things below go together. Think about why. **Group** them in the chart, and then write to tell about why they are a group.

Group 1	Group 2	Group 3
1. _____	1. _____	1. _____
2. _____	2. _____	2. _____
3. _____	3. _____	3. _____
4. _____	4. _____	4. _____
Why?	**Why?**	**Why?**
_____ _____ _____	_____ _____ _____	_____ _____ _____

flower	juice	plant	hot dog
bread	apple	grass	rain
carrot	milk	lake	tree

Grouping Objects

Think about how these objects in the sky are the same. Think about how they are different. **Categorize** them, or put them into two groups. Draw a ◯ around the objects in one group. Draw a ▢ around the objects in the other group.

1.

Write to tell about each group.

2. _____

_____

3. _____

_____

Tools That Solve Problems

Scientists make and use tools to **solve** problems. When you solve, you find an answer to a problem. Read about the problems below. Then match each problem to the tool that solves it.

1. Something is too small for us to see closely.

2. We don't know how much something weighs.

3. Something is too far away for us to see well.

4. We don't know how long something is.

5. Something could splash in our eyes and hurt our eyes.

Using Thermometers

Read. Then answer the items.

A thermometer is a tool. It shows how hot or how cold things are. Thermometers help people in many ways.

A thermometer can show you if the air outside is hot or cold. Then you can choose what clothes to wear.

A thermometer can show you how hot food is. Then you will know when the food is finished cooking.

A thermometer can tell you how hot your body is. Then you will know if you are sick.

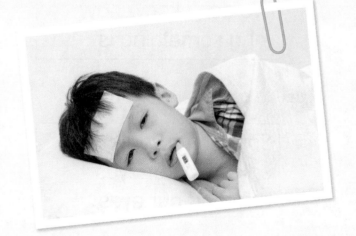

SKILLS
Demonstrate understanding of how
thermometers are used; Write to explain

Fill in the circle by the correct answer.
Then answer the questions.

1. A thermometer can show you how _____.

   Ⓐ much it rained

   Ⓑ fast the air is moving

   Ⓒ hot or cold the air is

2. A thermometer is a _____.

   Ⓐ tool   Ⓑ toy   Ⓒ temperature

3. In what places around a home are thermometers used?

   _____

4. Do people really need to use thermometers?
   Explain why or why not.

   _____

   _____

5. Have you ever seen or used a thermometer? Tell about it.

   _____

   _____

Science Jobs

People who do science jobs are called **scientists**.
Look at the pictures. Read the words that tell about
science jobs that people do. Then answer the questions.

Working with Science

Ocean Science
oceans, water, animals, plants

Rock Science
rocks, stones, land, minerals

Plant Science
plant life, seeds

Computer Science
computers, code, programs

Dinosaur Science
dinosaurs, bones, fossils

Animal Science
animals, health, medicine

SKILLS
Demonstrate visual literacy; Use inference;
Write to inform

Fill in the circles by the correct answers.
Then write an answer to the question.

1. Which scientist would try to find out why oceans change?

   ○ plant scientist

   ○ ocean scientist

   ○ rock scientist

2. Which 2 scientists would try to find out the plants dinosaurs ate? Fill in 2 circles.

   ○ plant scientist   ○ dinosaur scientist

   ○ ocean scientist   ○ animal scientist

   ○ rock scientist   ○ computer scientist

3. Which scientist would try to find out why mountains change?

   ○ animal scientist

   ○ ocean scientist

   ○ rock scientist

4. Which kind of scientist would you want to be? Tell why.

   _____

   _____

Being a Vet

Read about vets. They are scientists who help solve problems for animals. Then answer the items.

Being a Vet

It is fun to work with science. Do you like animals? Do you like pets? If so, you could be a veterinarian one day. Veterinarians, or vets, study animals. There are vets for small animals. There are vets for large animals. All vets are animal scientists.

small animals

Vets help animals in many ways. Sometimes, an animal gets sick. The vet will work to learn why the animal isn't feeling well. The vet can give the animal medicine. Vets also help pet owners keep their animals healthy.

large animals

Even a cat might need to go on a diet sometimes!

Vets are scientists who care about pets and their owners. They work hard to help all kinds of animals.

SKILLS
Demonstrate visual literacy; Demonstrate
reading comprehension; Write to explain

Answer the items.

1. Veterinarians are scientists who study _____.

   Ⓐ rocks

   Ⓑ oceans

   Ⓒ animals

2. A vet for large animals could _____.

   Ⓐ give medicine to a horse

   Ⓑ put a cat on a diet

   Ⓒ help a sick bird

3. Name two kinds of animals that a vet could help.

   _____

4. Tell how vets solve problems.

   _____

   _____

5. Do you think vets help only animals? Or do vets help people, too? Tell why you think so.

   _____

   _____

Know Living Things

Look at the pictures. Circle each living thing.

1.

Write two things that are true about **all** living things.

2. _____

_____

3. _____

_____

Grouping Animals

Group the animals. Think about how some of the animals are the same. Write the animal names in the chart. Then answer the question.

Group 1	Group 2	Group 3
1. _____	1. _____	1. _____
2. _____	2. _____	2. _____
3. _____	3. _____	3. _____
4. _____	4. _____	4. _____

What does each group have in common?

Group 1	Group 2	Group 3
_____	_____	_____
_____	_____	_____

duck	bear	whale	dog
owl	fish	lion	bird
sea horse	cat	eagle	dolphin

What Animal Is It?

All dogs look alike in some ways. In other ways they look different. That is how all animals are. This is because animals of the same kind have most of the same body parts. Look at each shadow below. Write what animal you think it is and why.

1.

This is the shadow of _____

because _____

_____.

2.

This is the shadow of _____

because _____

_____.

3.

This is the shadow of _____

because _____

_____.

Plants Can Look Different

The flowers in the picture are all the same kind.
They are buttercups. Look at the picture.
Then answer the items.

1. Write one way that the buttercups all look the same.

   _____

   _____

2. Write one way that the buttercups look different from each other.

   _____

   _____

How Plants Look

When people are born, they look a little bit like their parents. But people also look a little bit different from their parents. This is also how plants are. Plants look a little bit like their parent plants because they have the same plant parts. But plants can look different in some ways. Look at the pictures. Then answer the items.

1. Both of the pictures show the same kind of cactus. They grow in the same desert, so they might be related. Write one way they look alike.

   _____

   _____

2. Write one way they look different.

   _____

   _____

Animals and Their Parents

Look at the pictures of the animal mothers and their babies. Then answer the questions.

1. Do animals have the same body parts as their parents? Tell how you know.

_____

_____

_____

2. Do all of the animals in the pictures look exactly the same as their parents? Tell what you think and why.

_____

_____

_____

Animal Traits Can Help People

All animals have **traits**. A trait is a part or a detail that makes something special or different. A trait of dogs is that they have a strong sense of smell. A trait of toads is that they have bumpy skin. Read about the animal traits below, and look at the pictures. Then answer the questions.

1.

   Millipedes make a bad smell to keep dangerous animals away.

Which of these things that people do is like what millipedes do?

○ We put bug spray on ourselves because the smell keeps bugs off us.

○ We wear shoes to protect our feet.

2.

   Pelicans use the deep pouches in their bills to scoop up fish.

Which of these things that people do is like what pelicans do?

○ We buy fish from a store.

○ We use nets to scoop up fish from the ocean.

Plants and fruits have **traits** like animals do. A trait of roses is that they have thorns. A trait of apples is that they have skin. Read about the traits below, and look at the pictures. Then answer the questions.

1.

   The hard walnut shell protects the walnut.

   What do people use that works the same way as the walnut shell?

   ○ A pillow helps our heads feel good.

   ○ A hard bike helmet protects our heads.

2.

   A pitcher plant makes a juice that smells sweet and brings bugs. Then the plant eats the bugs.

   What do people use that works the same way as the plant's juice?

   ○ We use bait to catch fish to eat.

   ○ We use soap so we smell good.

Animal Patterns

A **pattern** is something that repeats. When we see a pattern, we know what will come next. We can see shape patterns, number patterns, and letter patterns. We can also see patterns in what animals do. Animals do the same things over and over again. This helps them to live.

Write a word from the box to finish each sentence about an animal pattern.

> eats   sleeps   hunts   cries   drinks

1. When a lion _____, it gets food to eat.

2. When a baby elephant _____, its mom comes to help.

3. When a koala _____, it does not feel tired anymore.

4. When a bird _____, it gets energy so it can move.

5. When a deer _____ water, it feels cool and not too hot.

Top Student • EMC 9321 • © Evan-Moor Corp.

People Patterns

Read. Then answer the questions.

We can see patterns in what people do. Think about a parent and baby. A baby does the same things over and over again. A parent does, too. When a baby feels hungry, the baby cries. When the baby cries, the parent gives the baby food. Then the baby is full. The next time the baby feels hungry, he or she will cry again. Then the parent will give the baby food again. The baby repeats a lot of patterns. When the baby falls down, the baby cries. Then the parent comes to help the baby.

Parents repeat patterns, too. When the parent rocks the baby, the baby falls asleep. When the parent makes funny faces, the baby laughs. Parents and babies repeat patterns. These patterns help the baby to live and grow.

1. Why do parents repeat patterns?

_____

_____

2. Why do babies repeat patterns?

_____

_____

How Earth Moves

Read. Then answer the items.

   Earth spins all the way around, once every day. Each day, the sun and moon seem to move across the sky. But they are not moving. Earth is! Every time Earth spins, we have a new day. As Earth spins, the side we live on turns toward the sun. We see the sun, and it is daytime. Earth keeps rotating all day. When the side we live on turns away from the sun, it becomes dark. It is night, and we see the stars. Stars give off their own light. We see the moon shining at night. The moon is made of rock. It does not make its own light. Light from the sun makes the moon shine brightly. The sun is a star, but we do not see it at night because we are turned away from it. It is the closest star to Earth. We need the sun because it gives us light and heat.

   As Earth spins all day, it also moves around the sun. It does both at the same time! The part of Earth that is tilted toward the sun gets more sunshine. That is 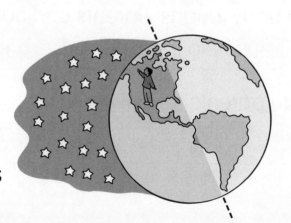 when it is summer. We get more sunshine during summer. That is why it is hotter. That is also why the days are longer. When it is winter, part of Earth is tilted away from the sun. The days are colder, and it gets dark earlier.

Answer the items.

1. Why does it seem like the sun and the moon move across the sky? Tell about it.

   _____

   _____

   _____

2. Do we get more daylight in winter or in summer? Tell why in your answer.

   _____

   _____

   _____

3. Why does the moon shine brightly at night?

   ○ The moon makes its own light.

   ○ The moon is made of rock.

   ○ The sun's light makes the moon shine.

What Would You Do?

SKILLS
Social and Emotional Learning:
Demonstrate self-reflection; Express your
opinion; Demonstrate social awareness

Remember that scientists solve problems. Answer the items about problems that scientists could help solve.

1. If you were a scientist who could solve any problem in the world, which problem would you want to solve the **most**?

   ○ animals being sick   ○ oceans being polluted

   ○ people being sick   ○ computer problems

   Now tell why.

   _____

   _____

2. Scientists care about the problems people have. They also care about animals and Earth. Do you think you would like to be a scientist and help people?

   ○ yes   ○ no

   Now tell why.

   _____

   _____

3. In which ways would you like to learn about science? Circle all the ways.

   watching TV   reading a book

   on the computer   watching a movie

STEM

Science
Technology
Engineering
Math

Task: Read about why shade is important. Then make something that will give shade to 2 small toys.

Read the text and look at the pictures and labels.

Shade from the Sun's Energy

The sun gives us light and energy that help us live and grow. We can see the energy as light. We can feel the energy as heat. But the sun's light and heat are powerful. Too much sunlight can hurt living things. It can hurt our eyes, burn our skin, and make us too hot. We must stay safe in the sun.

Light travels in a straight line. It can shine through some things, like a glass window or water. Light cannot shine through other things, like wood, a rock, or a ball. When light cannot move through something, you can see a **shadow**. A shadow is a dark shape that appears when an object blocks light. The darkness from the shadow is called **shade**. It helps keep you cool and safe from the sun's light.

A great place to find shade is under a tree. The branches and leaves of a tree grow out from the thick trunk. Light cannot shine through wood or leaves, so a shadow appears in the shape of the tree. You can also stand under an umbrella to get shade. The shade from a tree or an umbrella helps you stay safe on a sunny day.

SKILL
Understand that shade helps keep
people safe from the sun's light

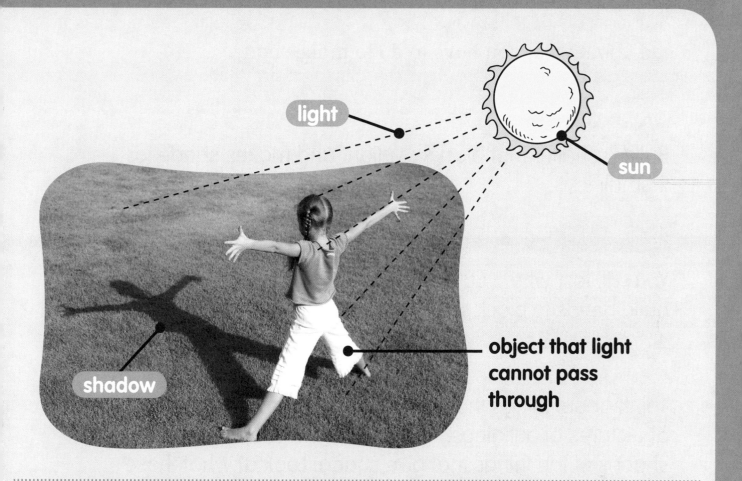

light

sun

shadow

object that light
cannot pass
through

leaves

branch

shade

shadow

STEM Challenge: Making Shade

Read about what you have to do to make shade.

Challenge

Build a shelter that blocks sunlight and makes shade for 2 small toys.

Testable Goals

You will test what you built to see if it works. The shelter you build needs to block sunlight.

Research

Think about things that give shade on a sunny day. Look at pictures of buildings, trees, and umbrellas. Look at the shapes of the things that give shade. Look at what these things are made out of.

Brainstorm

Think about the different things that give shade. Think about what you will build to block light and make shade. Then draw a picture in the box on the next page of what you want your shelter to look like.

Top Student • EMC 9321 • © Evan-Moor Corp.

SKILLS
Conduct research; Draw to design a
solution; Draw to communicate information

Suggested Materials List

- [ ] glue
- [ ] tape
- [ ] string
- [ ] scissors
- [ ] cardboard
- [ ] paper
- [ ] plastic wrap
- [ ] wax paper
- [ ] craft sticks
- [ ] paper towel rolls
- [ ] straws
- [ ] ruler
- [ ] two small toys
- [ ] sunlight or flashlight

Design Process: Making Shade

Read about the design process for this challenge.

Design Process

 Plan: Think about the things you have. How can you use them to build something that blocks light and gives shade to small toys?

 Create: Look at the design you drew. Then use the things you have to build something that blocks light.

 Test: Place two small toys under what you built. Does it stay up? Does light shine through it?

 How Did It Work?: Think about what happened during your tests. Did your design work? What can you do to make it better? Plan, create, and test until you are happy with your shelter.

Follow the design process to build a shelter and test it.

 Plan: Write about your design. Tell what things you will use. Then draw your design.

 Create

 Test: Write about or draw to show what happened when you did your tests.

 How Did It Work?: Write what you think.

STEM Challenge: Maraca Music

Task: Read about maracas and sound. Then make 2 maracas that make different sounds.

Read the text and look at the pictures and labels.

Vibrations and Music

Sounds are all around us. A bird chirps, a bell rings, and a drum goes boom! But how are sounds made? Sound comes from vibrations. When something **vibrates**, or shakes, it moves back and forth. The vibrations make **sound waves**. The sound waves move through the air and into your ear.

Some sound waves are musical. You can hear them when an instrument is played. When you hit a drum or pluck a guitar string, it vibrates. A **maraca** is an instrument that makes a sound when you shake it. Some maracas are made from a large round fruit called a gourd. The fruit has a hard shell. The hard shell is filled with seeds or pebbles. When you shake the maraca, the seeds or pebbles hit the hard shell. Sound waves move through the air, and people hear the sound of the maraca.

Not all maracas sound the same. A maraca filled with seeds sounds different from a maraca filled with pebbles. Shaking the maraca hard can make a loud sound. Shaking a maraca softly makes a softer sound.

Top Student • EMC 9321 • © Evan-Moor Corp.

Vibrations make sound waves. You can hear sound waves, but you cannot see them.

Hitting a drum makes vibrations.

Hard outside

Maracas made from a gourd

Handle for easy shaking

Seeds inside

STEM Challenge: Maraca Music

Read about what you have to do to make maracas.

Challenge

Make 2 maracas that have different sounds.

Testable Goals

You will test what you made to see if it works. When you shake the maracas, you should hear two different sounds.

Research

Look at pictures of maracas. Look at the shape of the maracas and what they are made from. Think about how the things inside the maracas make a certain sound.

Brainstorm

Think about how different maracas have different sounds. Think about the sounds you want your maracas to have. Then draw a picture in the box on the next page of the maracas you will make and what you will put in them.

STEM Challenge: Maraca Music

Follow the design process to make maracas and test them.

 Plan: Write about your design. Tell what things you will use. Then draw your design.

 Create

 Test: Write about or draw to show what happened when you did your tests.

 How Did It Work?: Write what you think.

How Do You Feel?

Complete the items.

1. You did a STEM challenge to make shade. Circle the words that tell what you think about the challenge. You can circle as many words as you want.

   | fun   easy   hard   not fun   too hard   too easy |

2. Do you like making things with your hands? Tell why or why not.

   _____

   _____

   _____

3. Do you like it better when you work with a group or by yourself? Tell why.

   _____

   _____

   _____

Top Student • EMC 9321 • © Evan-Moor Corp.

SKILLS
Social and Emotional Learning:
Evaluate your feelings; Give your opinion;
Write to explain

4. Think about the shelter you built. What if you were working with another person, and he or she wanted to make the shelter in a different way than you. What would you say to that person? Write one sentence.

_____

_____

5. If you were able to pick two friends to work on building a shelter with you, who would you choose?

_____

_____

Now write to tell why you would choose each person.

_____

_____

_____

_____

_____

Working Together

SKILLS
Social and Emotional Learning:
Demonstrate social awareness: Describe
positive behaviors

Pretend this robot is going to help you with your next STEM Challenge. Give it a name. Then write four things that are important for it to know about working together on a project. Last, color the robot.

_____
robot's name

1. _____

2. _____

3. _____

4. _____

Top Student • EMC 9321 • © Evan-Moor Corp.

Social Studies

Find Mom!

Clara is looking for her mom all over the neighborhood.
Follow the clues to find where she is. Then answer the question.

- She is **east** of the police station.
- She is **west** of the market.
- She is **south** of the gas station.
- She is **north** of the airport.

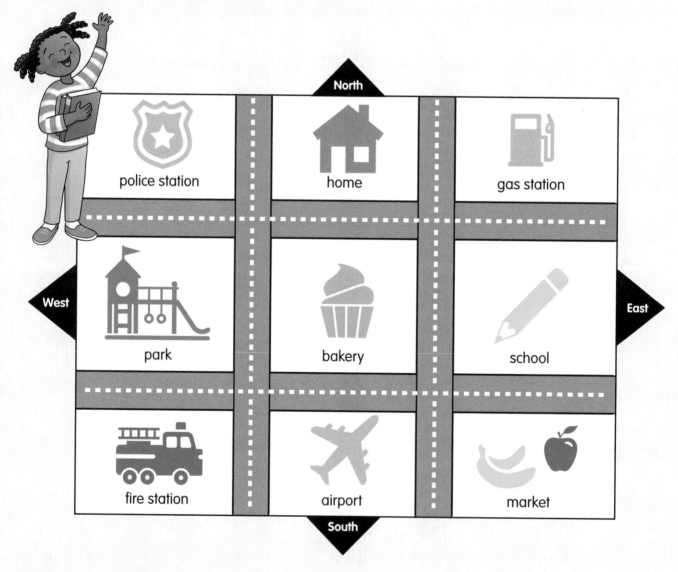

Where is Clara's mom?

_____

See the Playground from Above

Pretend you were a bird flying over the playground.
You would see parts of the playground from above.
Match the parts of the playground to the pictures
that show them from above.

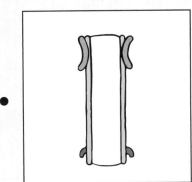

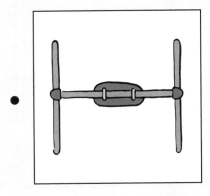

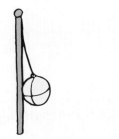

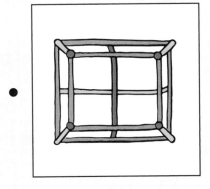

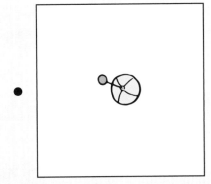

Rules I Follow

Think about rules you follow every day. Some rules are for safety. Some rules are for good manners. People follow rules at school, at home, at stores, and at other places. Write three rules that you always follow.

1. _____

2. _____

3. _____

Choose one rule. Draw a picture to **give an example** of someone breaking the rule. Draw a picture to **give an example** of someone following the rule.

4. Breaking a rule

5. Following a rule

People Make Rules

The people who live in Ann's neighborhood are making a list of six rules. **Decide** which rules are most important.

Neighborhood Rules

1.   4.

2.   5.

3.   6.

1. Make a ✔ beside the six rules you think should be on the list.

Keep the park clean. ☐   Keep dogs on a leash. ☐

Drive the speed limit. ☐   Use the crosswalks. ☐

Walk to school. ☐   Wear a bike helmet. ☐

Wear green shoes. ☐   Help save water. ☐

Wave to people. ☐   Be quiet after 9:00 at night. ☐

2. Find a rule that you did <u>not</u> ✔. Why didn't you choose it?

_____

_____

What Is Voting?

Read. Then answer the items.

Lots of people vote. People in a country can vote for a president. Students in a classroom can vote about what to play. People can vote for their favorite songs. There are lots of things to vote for. But what is **voting**?

When you vote, you choose something. Different people choose different things. At the end of the voting, we see how many people voted for each choice.

Voting is a way to say what you want to happen. Sometimes people vote for a person to do a job. Sometimes family members vote on what to have for dinner. Sometimes students vote on what book to read as a class. Everybody can vote. Some people vote on a computer. Some people vote by writing what they choose. In a classroom, the students can vote by raising their hands.

People vote to choose who will be president or mayor. People vote to choose other government workers. Remember, voting is a way to say what you want to happen!

What should we read today?

Book 1   Book 2

   ⵊⵊⵊⵊ ⵊⵊ   ⵊⵊⵊⵊ ⵊⵊⵊⵊ

Top Student • EMC 9321 • © Evan-Moor Corp.

Answer the items.

1. Did you ever vote for something at school or at home?

   ○ yes   ○ no

2. Pretend that your family is going to watch a movie. Everyone in your family will vote. Which kind of movie will you vote for?

   ○ scary   ○ funny   ○ adventure

3. Write one thing that you would like to vote for.

   _____

Finish the sentence.

4. Voting is important because it _____.

   ○ is not fair

   ○ helps everyone say what they want

   ○ makes it so nobody likes what happens

Answer the question.

5. Do you think voting is a good thing to do? Tell why or why not.

   _____

   _____

People Make Rules

Read. Think about what each person says.
Then tell who you would vote for and why.

Two students want to be the class ball monitor.
Ms. Simas has asked the class to vote. Both students
explained why they would be the best ball monitor.

✓ **Vote for Vinny**

If I am the ball monitor, I will choose
fun games for us to play. I will bring out
different kinds of balls. I will make sure
there are enough balls for everyone.

✓ **Vote for Krissy**

If I am the ball monitor, I will take care of
the balls. I will see that no one is left out
of any games. I will make sure we come
back to class on time.

I would vote for _____ for ball monitor

because _____

_____.

What Is Money?

Read.

     People use money. We work to get money. Then we spend it, or use it, to buy things. We pay money for things like clothes, food, and toys. We also give money to people who do services, or jobs. People pay money to go on rides at theme parks. People pay money to ride on airplanes. Some children do chores at home to get money. Money can be coins or bills. Money is an important reason why people work.

Answer the items.

1. Write a list of 3 things that people can buy with money.

_____

_____

2. Do you think people would want to do work if they didn't get money for their work? Tell why.

_____

_____

Do You Use Money?

SKILLS
Apply real-world experience and knowledge
to answer questions; Give your opinion;
Write to explain

Read. Think about what you do with money.

> Do you have any money?
> If you do, did you work for it?
> Or did someone give it to you?
> Will you buy something with your money?
> Or will you save it?

Fill in the circle to tell what you think. Then answer the item.

1. It is good to save all of your money. You may need it for something important in the future.

   ○ I agree.
   ○ I do not agree.

2. Tell why you agree or do not agree.

   _____

   _____

   _____

3. It is good to save some of your money and use some of your money to buy things.

   ○ I agree.
   ○ I do not agree.

4. Tell why you agree or do not agree.

   _____

   _____

   _____

My Shop

Read.

Goods are things that people sell. Goods are grown or made. A **service** is work that someone does for someone else.

Apples are grown.

Toys are made.

A doctor helps you feel better.

A barber cuts hair.

Create your own shop. Tell about it.

1. Draw a picture of your shop that sells **goods**.

   The goods I sell at my shop

   are _____.

   They cost _____.

2. Draw a picture of your **service**.

   The service I give is

   _____.

   It costs _____.

What Is History?

Read. Then answer the items.

Life Long Ago

History is what happened long ago. We can learn about history. We can learn about the people. We can learn about places. We can learn many things by studying the past.

You can study people who lived long ago. Ask questions about them. Ask about how they lived. You can find some answers to your questions in history books. You can find other answers on the Internet.

You can also study objects from the past. Old objects can help you learn more about how people lived. Go to a museum. You can see objects from history there. Museums are a good way to learn about the past.

© Remi Mathis (2011)

**This cup is about 3,000 years old.
It is in a museum in the United States.**

Top Student • EMC 9321 • © Evan-Moor Corp.

Fill in the circle by the correct answer.
Then answer the questions.

1. History is what happened in the _____.

   Ⓐ past

   Ⓑ present

   Ⓒ future

2. You can find objects from history in a _____.

   Ⓐ timeline

   Ⓑ new place

   Ⓒ museum

3. What can you learn from looking at an old object?

   Ⓐ what kinds of objects people used long ago

   Ⓑ what kinds of objects people use today

   Ⓒ how to find a museum

4. Write one question you have about history.

   _____

   _____

5. Would it have been fun to live a long time ago?   yes   no
   Tell why.

   _____

Objects in a Museum

SKILLS
Discriminate between facts and opinions;
Draw to inform; Write to inform

Pretend you are in a museum. Read some **facts** and **opinions** about the objects. Draw a line under each fact.

1.

This is a pretty frame. It was made in 1899. It is made of wood.

2.

This rocking horse was made in 1920. It is a beautiful horse. Only 20 of them were made.

Now draw a picture of something you would like to see in a museum. Write facts about it.

3.

_____

_____

_____

_____

★ **Facts** tell information that is completely true.
Opinions tell what someone thinks. Different people can have different opinions about the same thing.

Top Student • EMC 9321 • © Evan-Moor Corp.

Class Field Trip

Read and follow the directions.

Pretend you are going on a class field trip. Your teacher will take your class to a place where everyone wants to go. Where should you go? Do you want to go to a museum? Do you want to go see a musical? Do you want to go to a farm? Your classmate Joy wants to go to the zoo. She made a poster.

Let's go to the **ZOO!** We can learn about elephants and lions!

Think about where you would like to go. Then draw a poster that will get your other classmates to want to go there, too.

Objects Change with Time

Many things we use change over time.
Read and follow the directions.

First, someone gets an idea and makes something new.
Later on, other people make the same thing better.
Look at the ways people have traveled.

1. **Order** the photos from **first** to **last** to show how traveling has changed. Draw a line from the year to its picture.

1890   1915   1950   2020

2. How did you decide which one was second?

_____

Invent Something New

When you **invent**, you make something that has never been made before. An **invention** is something that is different from everything that came before it. Read and look at the pictures.

People rode in covered wagons in the past.

Now people ride in cars.

Invent a new way for people to travel. Tell about it.

1. Draw a picture of your new way to travel.

2. What is your new idea called?

   It is called _____

   _____.

3. Does your new idea travel in the air? In the water? On land?

   It travels _____

   _____.

Inventions

Read about the inventions. Then answer the items.

Ballpoint Pens

For hundreds of years, people used quill pens. A quill is a bird feather. To write, a person dipped the quill in ink. It was very messy. Then someone made fountain pens. The ends were metal. People dipped the ends in ink to write. It was also messy. Finally, a man made a ballpoint pen. The end had a metal ball it in. The pen held ink inside. It came out only when someone used the pen to write. It was not messy. We use these pens a lot today.

Phones

The first phones were made hundreds of years ago. They were not like the cellphones we use today. Later, phones had wires. The wires plugged into the wall. Many people still use these phones today. Some people wanted to be able to talk on the phone and move around. You cannot do this with a phone that is plugged in. So someone invented the cellphone. The first cellphones did not have cameras or touch screens.

Fill in the circle to finish the sentences.

1. Both of the inventions _____.
   ○ are the same as they were hundreds of years ago
   ○ went through lots of changes over time

2. Both of the inventions _____.
   ○ made something work better
   ○ made something worse

3. Both of the inventions will probably _____.
   ○ stay the same
   ○ change

Draw an invention for something you think we need today.

Different Place, Different Custom

People in different places do some things differently.
That is what makes the world so interesting!
Read the facts in the boxes. Look at the photos.
Then write the name of the country under each photo.

A town in **Thailand** celebrates Monkey Buffet Festival. The people feed monkeys lots of fresh fruit.

In **Australia**, Aboriginal Australians wear face and body paints.

In **Tanzania**, women carry containers on their heads.

In **India**, many people eat with their hands every day.

_____

_____

_____

_____

Himba Huts

SKILLS
Demonstrate visual literacy; Make
inferences; Write to compare and contrast

Read and look at the photos. Then answer the questions.

People around the world build homes using things
around them. The Himba people in Africa live in huts.

1. What do you think the Himba people use to make
the huts?

_____

2. How are these two huts different from each other?

_____

_____

3. How is this home different from yours?

_____

_____

The Holi Festival

Read the text.
Then answer the items.

Holi is a colorful holiday.

People all over the world like to welcome spring. They are happy to leave the dark winter behind. Holi is a spring festival in India. This festival comes from ancient times. One ancient story tells about a prince who was saved from a bonfire. The story tells how good won over evil. That is why people light bonfires on the night before Holi. They dance and sing.

Holi is also called the Festival of Colors. It is wise to dress in old clothes to celebrate Holi. That is because people in the streets spray colors at each other. They toss colorful powders and squirt colored water. Everyone laughs and has a good time. And everyone gets covered in colors! It does not matter if you are young or old. It does not matter if you are rich or poor. It does not matter if you are a friend or a stranger. No one minds because it is all in good fun!

Answer the items about the text.

1. Holi is a festival where people toss _____.
   Ⓐ rice
   Ⓑ flowers
   Ⓒ powders

2. What do you think the word **wise** means in the text?
   Ⓐ sad
   Ⓑ smart
   Ⓒ poor

3. Why is Holi also called the Festival of Colors?

   _____

   _____

4. What do people do to show they are happy that good won over evil?

   _____

   _____

What Do You Celebrate?

You have read about the Holi Festival in India. Now think about celebrations you have been a part of. Answer the items below.

1. Write the name of a holiday or a festival that you have celebrated.

   _____

2. Write an **X** in the box if the sentence tells something you did when you celebrated.

   ☐ I ate special foods.   ☐ I wore special clothes.

   ☐ I stayed up later   ☐ I saw a parade or
      than I usually do.   fireworks.

   ☐ I celebrated with family.   ☐ I played special games.

   ☐ I watched a special movie. ☐ I had a special drink.

3. Draw a picture of yourself celebrating.
   You can draw your family and friends celebrating, too.

Birthday Celebrations Around the World

People do things every year to celebrate birthdays. What people do and how they do it changes from country to county. Read about three birthday traditions in three different countries.

In Norway, people eat chocolate cake on their birthdays.

In Mexico, people hit a piñata on their birthdays.

In the Philippines, people eat noodles for a long life on their birthdays.

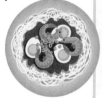

Look at the picture of the birthday celebration.
Find 9 things that don't belong in the picture. Circle them.

Mindful Moments

track 2

Listen to the audio

For students in China

Stand up.

Gently wiggle your body.

Wiggle your hands.

Wiggle your fingers, very gently.

Now wiggle your toes.

Slowly bring your hands up high.

Slowly bring your hands down low.

Now stand still.

Breathe in as you count to 3.

Breathe out as you count to 3.

Now stand on **1** foot for as long as you can.

Put your hands out to the sides.

Think about the foot you are standing on. How does it feel? How does your leg feel?

Now put your foot back on the ground.

Take a deep breath in through your nose and let it out through your mouth.

SEL

Social and Emotional Learning

Words Tell About People

Read the words below. Think about your friends and family. Do any of these words tell about them? Use these words or words of your own to tell about one family member and one friend. Then draw a picture or a symbol to show how you feel about that person.

nice	helpful	shy	smart
strong	giving	happy	quiet
funny	caring	gentle	kind

family

Draw.

1. These words tell about _____.

_____ _____

_____ _____

friend

Draw.

2. These words tell about _____.

_____ _____

_____ _____

Words and Feelings

Everybody has feelings. We can think about other people's feelings when we talk and do things.

Read the sentences below. Look at the pictures.
Then draw a line to match the words to the picture that shows how someone might feel.

You say something mean.

You do something nice for someone.

You help someone.

You do not answer when someone talks to you.

You say something nice.

You yell at someone.

What I Can Do

Draw a picture of yourself in the circle.
Then write answers in the boxes.

Write something
that you like to do.

Write something
that you do well.

Tell about a nice thing
you have done.

Tell why you are a good
friend.

I Can Help

SKILLS
Understand what actions are helpful;
Reflect on how actions impact others

Write what you can do to help.
Use the words in the box or
words of your own.

- give them a hug
- tell them a story
- make them a card
- play a game with them
- make them a snack
- help them do something

1. This is what I can do to help my parents.

   I can _____.

   I can _____.

2. This is what I can do to help my brothers or sisters.

   I can _____.

   I can _____.

3. This is what I can do to help my friends.

   I can _____.

   I can _____.

Things I Can Do

Read the words in the box.
Do they tell something that you
should do or **should not do**?
Write the words in the chart.

- scream when you feel mad
- talk loudly when someone else is already talking
- wait for someone else to finish talking before you talk
- throw something when you feel mad
- think about other people's feelings
- think about why you feel mad

Should Do	Should Not Do
1. _____	4. _____
2. _____	5. _____
3. _____	6. _____

Other People and Me

Read the sentence. Write an answer.

1. Write one way that you are nice to others.

   _____

   _____

2. Write one nice thing that someone did for you.

   _____

   _____

3. Write one thing that makes you sad or mad sometimes.

   _____

   _____

4. Write one thing that makes you feel happy.

   _____

   _____

5. Draw a picture of yourself doing something nice for someone.

I Show My Feelings!

Read the words in each box.
Then draw a picture of yourself in each box.

This is me when I'm happy.

This is me when I'm sad.

This is me when I'm grumpy.

This is me when I'm trying really hard.

What to Do?

Read. Then write what you think the children should do.

Every day, kids just like you have to make choices. They try to do the right thing.

1. Greg has a problem. He saw a boy in his class break a rule two days in a row. What should Greg do?

   _____

   _____

2. Mika has a problem. Her little sister keeps taking Mika's things without asking. What should Mika do?

   _____

   _____

3. Kylie and her older brother, Bob, walk to school together. They are late, so Bob wants to go through someone's backyard. What should Kylie do?

   _____

   _____

Give Someone Your Heart

Make a heart card for someone. Write an **adjective** to tell about the person you give your heart to.

What You Need

- shapes on page 337
- white, pink, red, or purple construction paper
- scissors
- glue
- pen or marker

What You Do

1. Cut out the shapes and square label.
2. Place the shapes on top of the construction paper. Trace around the shapes.
3. Cut the slits on the dashed line, and fold on the fold line.
4. Weave the two sections together.
5. Glue the end pieces.
6. Cut a small heart from scraps of paper. Glue it and the message inside the card.

Message

You are

_____ !

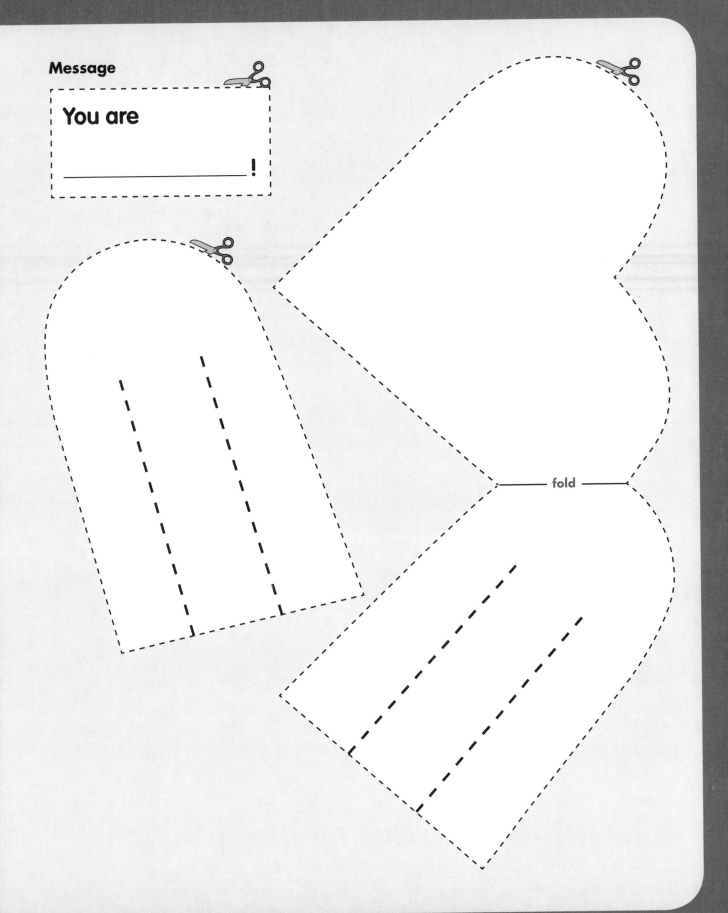

fold

338

Answer Key

Handwriting

Page 15

Items can be in any order:
carrots, milk, green beans,
cereal, pretzels, ice cream

Page 16

Answers will vary.

Phonics

Page 18

1. b	6. r
2. l	7. n
3. w	8. h
4. t	9. y
5. d	

Page 19

1. f	6. v
2. m	7. j
3. k	8. b
4. p	9. z
5. s	

Page 20

Circled words:
1. cent
5. circle
6. city

Page 21

Circled words:
2. gem
4. giant

Page 22

1. m	6. d
2. t	7. t
3. b	8. g
4. g	9. n
5. n	

Page 23

1. s	6. f
2. p	7. p
3. k	8. k
4. l	9. l
5. r	

Page 24

1. q
2. x
3. q

Page 25

1. s sound
2. z sound
3. s sound
4. s sound
5. z sound
6. s sound

Page 26

1. 2	4. 1
2. 1	5. 2
3. 2	6. 2

Page 27

1. yes	5. yes
2. no	6. no
3. yes	7. Answers will vary.
4. yes	

Page 28

1. yes	5. yes
2. no	6. yes
3. yes	7. Answers will vary.
4. no	

Page 29

1. yes	5. no
2. no	6. yes
3. yes	7. Answers will vary.
4. yes	

Page 30

1. yes	5. yes
2. no	6. no
3. yes	7. Answers will vary.
4. yes	

Page 31

1. yes	5. no
2. yes	6. yes
3. no	7. Answers will vary.
4. yes	

Page 32

1. i	6. i
2. a	7. a
3. i	8. i
4. a	9. a
5. a	

Page 33

1. e	6. o
2. o	7. e
3. o	8. o
4. o	9. e
5. e	

Page 34

1. mule	4. mule
2. blue	5. blue
3. blue	6. mule

Page 35

1. tub	6. fox
2. map	7. bed
3. jet	8. cup
4. bat	9. dog
5. rug	

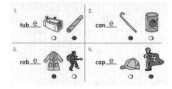

5. Answers will vary.

1. long i
2. long e
3. long e
4. long i
5. long e
6. long i
7. Answers will vary.

1. clay
2. rain
3. snail
4. train
5. spray
6. mail
7. Answers will vary.

1. peach
2. cheese
3. sleep
4. teeth
5. seal
6. feet
7. Answers will vary.

1. tie
2. high
3. night
4. thigh
5. fried
6. right
7. Answers will vary.

1. toe
2. toast
3. snow
4. soap
5. bow
6. boat
7. Answers will vary.

1. toy
2. soil
3. joy
4. boil
5. point
6. oil

1. mouth
2. house
3. clown
4. owl
5. cloud
6. crown

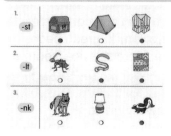

1. sp
2. sm
3. sk
4. sp
5. sk
6. sp
7. sk
8. sm
9. sk

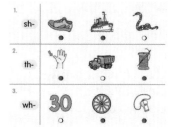

1. gl
2. pl
3. bl
4. pl
5. bl
6. gl
7. bl
8. gl
9. gl

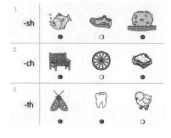

1. tr
2. gr
3. dr
4. gr
5. dr
6. tr
7. tr
8. dr
9. gr

1. -st
2. -lt
3. -nk

1. lf
2. mp
3. lf
4. nt
5. lf
6. nt
7. nt
8. mp
9. mp

1. cl
2. mp
3. tr
4. lt
5. st
6. br
7. lf
8. sp
9. sk

1. sh-
2. th-
3. wh-

1. -sh
2. -ch
3. -th

Page 56

Answers will vary.

Grammar and Punctuation

Page 60

1. boy
2. park
3. girl
4. book

Page 61

1. school
2. friend
3. cookie
4. teacher
5. cat

Page 62

Does the noun name **one** or **more than one**? Circle the correct picture.

1. kites
2. sister
3. rats
4. bird

5. hands
6. cows
7. teachers
8. hats

Page 63

1. boxes
2. bench
3. dish
4. glasses
5. dresses
6. foxes
7. bushes
8. beaches

Page 64

1. goose, geese
2. mouse, mice
3. child, children
4. man, men
5. tooth, teeth
6. men, women
7. children
8. geese

Page 65

1. fish
2. deer
3. men
4. mice
5. Drawings will vary but should show the correct number.

Page 66

1. Manny
2. Main Street
3. Buddy, Missy
4. Houston, Texas
5. Kara
6. Lark School

Page 67

1. Dad's
2. chair's
3. Ben's
4. park's
5. Mom's
6. bird's
7. Lisa's
8. the cat

Page 68

1. trees'
2. dogs'
3. girls'
4. cows'
5. cars'
6. boys'
7. ladybugs', bugs'

Page 69

1. little
2. three
3. hot
4. sweet

Page 70

1. ten
2. green
3. Bright
4. many
5. round
6. yellow
7. long
8. spotted

Page 71

1. clean
2. dirty
3. fluffy
4. wet
5. fishy
6. minty
7. squishy
8. furry

Page 72

1. humming
2. popping
3. minty
4. crunchy
5. moaning
6. salty
7. yummy
8. bubbling

Page 73

1. ugly
2. pretty
3. scary
4. upset
5. excited
6. playful
7. hard
8. wonderful

Page 74

1. longer
2. older
3. slower
4. shorter
5. smaller

Page 75

1. quickest
2. smartest
3. deepest
4. longest
5. shortest
6. coldest

Page 76

1. this
2. that
3. This
4. That
5. this
6. that

Page 77

1. these
2. these
3. those
4. those
5. these
6. those

Page 78

Correct sentences shown for numbers 1–3:
1. Danny found a crab.
2. Deeta steps over an ant.
3. Latifah sees the hawks flying.
4. the

Page 79

1. She
2. He
3. it
4. Answers will vary.

Page 80

1. him
2. us
3. them
4. Answers will vary.

Page 81

1. Sara's pencils are sharp; Her pencils are sharp.
2. Jake's pencils are sharp; His pencils are sharp.
3. Drake and Pam's pencils are sharp; Their pencils are sharp.
4. Pedro and your pencils are sharp; Your pencils are sharp.
5. The classroom's pencils are sharp; Its pencils are sharp.
6. Kristin and my pencils are sharp; Our pencils are sharp.

Page 82

1. Hers
2. His
3. theirs
4. yours
5. ours
6. Answers will vary.

Page 83

1. everything
2. Everyone
3. anything
4. anyone
5. everyone
6. Answers will vary.

Page 84

1. reads
2. rides
3. eat
4. play

Page 85

1. rings
2. stand
3. opens
4. sits
5. reads
6. picks
7. listen

8. play
9. writes
10. count

Page 86

1. is
2. are
3. are
4. are
5. is
6. are
7. is
8. is

Page 87

1. call
2. ask
3. says
4. wants
5. buys
6. makes
7. Answers will vary.

Page 88

1. moved
2. roared
3. clapped
4. followed
5. waved

Page 89

1. will make
2. will brush
3. will tie
4. will pack
5. will drive
6. Answers will vary.

Page 90

1. in
2. behind
3. under
4. on

Page 91

1. because
2. and
3. or
4. but
5. Answers will vary.

Top Student • EMC 9321 • © Evan-Moor Corp.

Page 92

Answers will vary.

Page 93

1. Answers will vary.
   End punctuation may very for some items below:
2. My grandpa is the best!
3. We learn about the weather.
4. What kinds of birds migrate?
5. I am so excited to go on the ride!

Page 94

1. Jamal's birthday party is on March 24, 2022.
2. Tanya got Jamal a gift on March 20, 2022.
3. Marie's birthday is on April 17, 2022.
4. Marie might have a party on April 19, 2022.
5. Her little brother Jared turns 2 on July 6, 2022.
6. Jamal's little sister turns 4 on September 3, 2022.
7.–8. Answers will vary.

Page 95

1. The
2. Do
3. Please
4. Answers will vary.

Page 96

1. Sunday
2. Monday
3. Tuesday
4. Wednesday
5. Thursday
6. Friday
7. Saturday
8. Answers will vary.

Page 97

1. April
2. July
3. December
4. Answers will vary.

Page 98

Answers will vary.

Spelling and Vocabulary

Page 100

1. Words grouped with **ate**: game, make, late, lake, tape, came, shake
   Words grouped with **hat**: sand, ran, hand, had, pat
2. make/lake
3. tape
4. game/came
5. pat

Page 101

1. Words grouped with **be**: he, need, we, bee, free, me, tree, see
   Words grouped with **pet**: fed, ten, get, let, bed, red, men
2. me
3. need
4. tree
5. sheep

Page 102

1. Words grouped with **dive**: ride, by, dime, nine, time, like, five
   Words grouped with **is**: it, big, did, sit, his, pig, six, dig
2. five
3. like
4. dime/time
5. by
6. ride
7. nine

Page 103

1. Words grouped with **no**: note, home, go, robe, so
   Words grouped with **hot**: not, hop, mop, dog, fox, on, top, stop
2. so/go
3. note
4. home
5. robe

Page 104

1. Words grouped with **flute**: chute, rule, rude, tune, tube, Luke
   Words grouped with **but**: cut, run, stuff, shut, duck, tub, stuck, fuss
2. pup
3. but/tub
4. bus
5. tub/but

Page 105

Answers may be in a different order:

1. ball
2. bell
3. hill
4. fell
5. fall
6. hill
7. ball
8. bell
9. fell
10. ball
11. bell
12. fall
13. fell
14. hill

Page 106

1. wish
2. shell
3. she
4. ship
5. dish

Circled words
are shown below:

ship	wish	she
shell	dish	ship
she	wish	shell

Page 107

1. five
2. like
3. ride
4. my
5. make
6. lake
7. came
8. game
9. you
10. do
11. robe
12. note
13. home
14. no
15. so
16. go

Page 108

1. bunny
2. mitten
3. happy
4. kitten
5. funny
6. penny
7. kitten
8. bunny
9. puppy
10. penny
11. mitten
12. bunny
13. happy
14. funny
15. little

Page 109

Answers will vary.

Page 110

Answers will vary.

Page 111

1. sunflower
2. baseball
3. airplane
4. playground
5. backpack
6. pancakes
7. football
8. butterfly

Page 112

1. baseball
2. sunshine
3. cupcakes
4. butterfly
5. rainbow
6. firefly
7. goldfish
8. backyard
9. Answers will vary.

Page 113

1. cent
2. sale
3. pear
4. bee
5. won
6. two

Page 114

1. huge, large
2. kind, caring
3. giggle, chuckle
4. upset, angry

Page 115

1. soft, hard
2. big, little
3. fast, slow
4. more, less
5. dark, light
6. young, old
7. old, young
8. soft, hard

Page 116

Examples will vary for items
below:

1. socks
2. rain
3. blanket
4. rock
5. grape
6. cracker
7. soup

Page 117

1. Words grouped with **People:**
doctor, baby, sister, teacher
Words grouped with **Animals:**
mouse, bird, lion, dog
2. Answers will vary.

Page 118

1. A bird that swims, duck
2. A small green animal that
hops, frog
3. An animal that has fins
and swims, fish
4. cow, A farm animal that
gives us milk
5. pig, A farm animal with
a curly tail
6. horse, A farm animal to
ride on

Top Student • EMC 9321 • © Evan-Moor Corp.

Page 119

1. pound
2. stare
3. run
4. leap
5. sing

Page 120

1. thrilled
2. huge
3. small
4. wonderful
5. awful

Page 121

1. tired
2. woke up
3. strong
4. dry land

Page 122

1. slide, a smooth object on a playground that people can move on top of easily
2. sink, to go down into something
3. chop, to cut into pieces
4. full, having as much or as many as can fit

Page 123

1. singer, a person who sings
2. cheerful, full of cheer
3. careless, without care
4. baker, a person who bakes
5. useless, without use
6. fearless, without fear
7. helpful, full of help

Page 124

1. opens, opened, opening; open
2. cooks, cooked, cooking; cook
3. talks, talked, talking; talk
4. cleans, cleaned, cleaning; clean

5. plays, played, playing; play
6. starts, started, starting, start
7. yells, yelled, yelling; yell
8. looks, looked, looking; look

Page 125

Answers will vary.

Page 126

Answers will vary.

Reading

Page 128

1. I need to wash my hair.
2. I wet my hair.
3. I put in shampoo.
4. I rinse my hair.

Page 129

1. First, dig a hole.
2. Last, put dirt around the tree.
3. Answers will vary.

Page 131

1. The mother sea turtle digs a hole in the sand.
2. The mother sea turtle lays eggs in the hole.
3. The baby sea turtles go into the water.
4. Drawings will vary.

Page 137

Explanations will vary for items below:
1. no
2. yes

Page 139

1. made up
2. talk

3. ant
4. frog

Page 141

1. people, plants, and animals
2.–3. Answers will vary.

Page 142

1. Do Not Feed the Birds
2. You May Feed the Animals
3. They help you know what to do.

Page 143

1. They show how many legs each living thing has.
2. yes

Page 145

1. girl
2. cat
3.–4. Answers will vary.

Page 146

1. The rabbit jumped off the sled.
2. Answers will vary.

Page 147

Crossed out sentences are shown:
1. I have long hair.
2. I have a sick pet at home.
3. It is warm outside.

Page 148

1. Sea otters eat a lot of different foods.
2. Answers will vary.

Page 149

1. Some bugs help plants.
2. A stinkbug eats smaller bugs that eat plants.
3. Answers will vary.

Page 150

1. the same and different
2.–3. Answers will vary.

Page 151

1. different
2. same
3. same
4. Drawings will vary.

Page 153

1.–2. Answers will vary.
3.

Page 154

1. the clouds are gray and thick
2. The sun shines in the rain.

Page 155

1. The air is very cold.
2. Children skate on the lake.
3. It is hard.

Page 157

1. She wants to go to the beach.
2. The crab wants help cleaning the beach.
3. The beach was clean.
4. Drawings will vary.

Page 158

1. rain
2. cold
3. cloudy

Page 159

1. food in his bowl
2. beach
3. Tyson's birthday

Page 160

1. snails
2. It leaves a trail of slime.
3. The snail tries to keep its body safe.

Page 161

Answers will vary.

Page 162

Answers will vary.

Writing

Page 164

Answers will vary.

Page 165

Answers will vary.

Page 166

1. family
2. happy
3. round

Page 167

1. The girl
2. laughs
3. The kids
4. barks
Completed sentences are shown:
5. The kite flies in the sky.
6. Boats are in the water.
7. The child picks up shells.
8. Beaches are made of sand.

Page 168

1. glad
2. hot
3. long
4. sweet
Answers may vary for items below:
5. happy   **7.** funny
6. hungry   **8.** quiet

Page 169

Order may vary for numbers 1–4:
1. Bees buzz.
2. Dogs dig.
3. Chicks chirp.
4. Skunks smell.
5. The fish swims.
6. A bird eats.

Page 170

Next and **Then** may be switched:
1. First
2. Then
3. Next
4. Last

Page 171

1. Order of words from left to right are shown: beginning, middle, end
2. Order of words from top to bottom are shown: beginning, middle, end

Page 172

Answers will vary.

Page 173

Answers will vary.

Page 174

Answers will vary.

Page 175

1. make-believe; Explanations will vary.
2. Sentence is circled.
3. Sentence is circled.
4. Sentence is not circled.
5. Answers will vary.

Page 176

1. Babies learn to crawl.
2. Babies learn to stand.
3. Babies learn to walk.
4. Babies learn to run.
5. Ⓑ

Page 177

Answers will vary.

Page 178

Answers will vary.

Page 179

Answers will vary.

Math

Page 186

1. 8
2. 9
3. 10

Page 187

Three of the following:
5 green/4 red
6 green/3 red
7 green/2 red
8 green/1 red

Page 188

Page 189

3 + 6 = 9   8 + 2 = 10
9 – 6 = 3   10 – 2 = 8
6 + 3 = 9   2 + 8 = 10
9 – 3 = 6   10 – 8 = 2

4 + 3 = 7   7 + 3 = 10
7 – 3 = 4   10 – 3 = 7
3 + 4 = 7   3 + 7 = 10
7 – 4 = 3   10 – 7 = 3

Page 190

1. 5 oranges
2. 3 lemons
3. 6 pears

Page 191

4. Problems will vary.

Page 192

Bears can be in any order:
- brown bear with red bow
- yellow bear with blue bow
- orange bear with purple bow

Page 193

The following should
be circled:

1. make **9**: 13 – 4, 6 + 3, 9 – 0,
   11 – 2
2. make **10**: 12 – 2, 3 + 7, 13 – 3,
   11 – 1, 6 + 4
3. make **11**: 4 + 7, 5 + 6, 11 – 0,
   9 + 2
4. make **12**: 8 + 4, 5 + 7, 12 – 0,
   6 + 6
5. make **13**: 11 + 2, 6 + 7, 10 + 3,
   4 + 9, 13 – 0

Page 194

1. 6 + 7 = 13, 13 birds
2. 8 – 4 = 4, 4 more
3. Problems will vary.

Page 195

1. Circle around the first 2
   shapes
2. A A B A A B A A B; circle
   around the first 3 shapes
3. A B C A B C A B C; circle
   around the first 3 shapes
4. A B B B A B B B; circle around
   the first 4 shapes
5. A B B A B B A B B; circle
   around the first 3 shapes
6. Drawings will vary.

Page 196

1. 7
2. 8
3. 9
4. 7
5. 8
6. 9

Page 197

Circled shapes:
second shape
third shape
first shape
third shape

Page 198

	12	13
15	14	19
18	17	16

Page 199

1. 12 campers
2. 14 birds
3. 15 fish
4. Word problems will vary.

Page 200

2. 4 tens 6 ones, 46
3. 5 tens 4 ones, 54
4. 2 tens 4 ones, 24
5. 4 tens 0 ones, 40
6. 3 tens 9 ones, 39
   Tables will vary.

Page 201

Balloons with these
numbers should be yellow:
19, 27, 49, 15

Remaining balloons should
be purple.

19 < 50   83 > 50
51 > 50   27 < 50
64 > 50   15 < 50
49 < 50   65 > 50

Page 202

one more – 12, 21, 37, 11, 43, 25, 50

one less – 20, 11, 34, 69, 85, 66, 99

ten more – 22, 29, 47, 17, 40, 56, 24

ten less – 19, 46, 72, 30, 25, 81, 67

Page 203

99, 98, 97, 96, 95, 93, 92, 91, 90

89, 88, 87, 86, 84, 83, 82, 81, 80,

79, 77, 76, 75, 74, 73, 72, 71

Page 204

15   27   37

1. the oldest
2. 10 years older
3. 12 years older

Page 205

1. dog
2. snake
3. cat and bird
4. Answers will vary.

Page 206

1. how students go to school
2. 3 more children
3. walk
4. 10 children

Page 207

30, 40, 50, 60, 70, 80, 90, 100

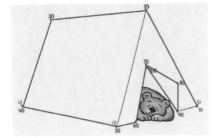

Page 208

1. 40
2. 90
3. 80
4. 30
5. 60
6. 70

Page 209

1.–3.

1	2	3	4	5	6	7	8	9	10
11	12	13	14	15	16	17	18	19	20
21	22	23	24	25	26	27	28	29	30
31	32	33	34	35	36	37	38	39	40
41	42	43	44	45	46	47	48	49	50
51	52	53	54	55	56	57	58	59	60
61	62	63	64	65	66	67	68	69	70
71	72	73	74	75	76	77	78	79	80
81	82	83	84	85	86	87	88	89	90
91	92	93	94	95	96	97	98	99	100

4. Descriptions will vary.

Page 210

48, 38, 38, 49, 53, 27, 48
a rooster

26, 53, 65, 48, 34, 27, 98
a turkey

Page 211

70, 12, 32, 11
35, 35, 35, 89, 13
54, 53, 35, 33, 31
34, 20, 35

Page 212

1. 15 + 12 = 27, 27 pounds
2. 10 + 10 + 6 = 26, 26 leaves
3. 30 + 8 = 38, 38 inches
4. 6 + 6 + 6 = 18, 18 porcupines

Page 213

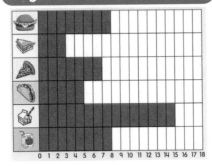

1.–2. Answers will vary.

Page 214

Graphs and responses will vary.

Page 215

Combinations will vary.

Page 217

2. 10¢ – 2 nickels circled
3. 15¢ – 1 dime and 1 nickel circled
4. 20¢ – 1 dime, 1 nickel, and 5 pennies circled
5. 35¢ – 3 dimes and 1 nickel circled OR 2 dimes and 3 nickels circled
6. 25¢ – 1 dime, 2 nickels, and 5 pennies circled

Page 218

1. 2¢ – 2 pennies should be drawn
2. 7¢ – 7 pennies OR 1 nickel and 2 pennies should be drawn
3. 6¢ – 6 pennies OR 1 nickel and 1 penny should be drawn
4. 3¢ – 3 pennies should be drawn
5. 5¢
6. 10¢
7. 10¢
8. 8¢
9. 4¢
10. 7¢
11. 7¢
12. 5¢

Page 219

1. 4 nickels
2. 35¢ more
3. 60¢

Page 220

1. 9:00
2. 11:30
3. 4:00
4. 2:30
5. 9:30
6. 6:00

Page 221

Answers will vary.

Page 222

Answers will vary.

Page 223

1. 12 fish, 15 shrimp
2. 25 more pounds
3. 17 seals
4. 98 minutes

Page 224

Bax   Zep   Ork   Ig

Page 225

1. 10 squares
2. 8 squares
3. 6 squares
4. 4 squares
5. Answers will vary.

Page 226

2. 11 – 4 = 7, 7 centimeters longer
3. 14 – 9 = 5, 5 centimeters longer
4. 6 – 3 = 3, 3 inches farther

Page 227

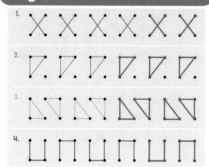

5. Patterns will vary.

Page 228

The following shapes should be drawn:

1. 4-sided shape (such as a rectangle, parallelogram, or trapezoid)
2. triangle
3. square OR rhombus
4. circle OR oval
5. They both have 4 sides and 4 corners.
6. A square has 4 sides that are the same length but a rectangle doesn't.

Page 229

1. The 3 triangles are circled.
2. The trapezoid and the rectangle above it are circled.
3. The half-circle, the triangle, and the rectangle on the right are circled.

Page 230

These shapes should be colored:

1. cylinder and sphere
2. cube, rectangular prism, and pyramid
3. both rectangular prisms, cube, and cylinder
4. sphere

Page 231

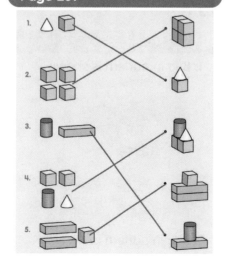

Page 232

1. The pizza and apple are circled.
2. The pizza and cracker are circled.
3. The pizza, pie, and cracker are circled.

Page 233

1. The sandwich is divided in half; an **X** is on one half.
2. The cheese is divided into thirds; an **X** is on one third.
3. The orange is divided in half; an **X** is on one half.
4. The cookie is divided into fourths; an **X** is on one fourth.

Page 234

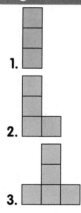

1.
2.
3.

Page 235

1. square box – 8 shells
2. round box – 12 shells

Page 236

Tallies and graphs will vary.

Page 237

Answers will vary.

Computer Science

1. No; Explanations will vary.
2. The computer will make a sound every time you turn it on.

Page 242

2. Stir up the cake mix.
3. Put it in the pan and bake it.
4. Put on the frosting and eat it up.

Page 243

Answers will vary.

Page 244

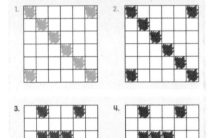

Page 245

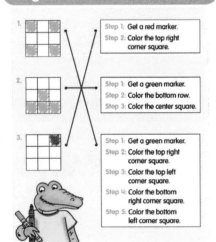

Page 246

Step 1: go right
Step 2: go down
Step 3: go right
Step 4: go up
Step 5: go right
Step 6: go down
Step 7: go right
Step 8: go down

Page 247

1. red
2. green
3. Answers will vary.

Page 248

1.

2. blue star

Page 249

1. E, H, X
2. Pictures shown are what students should draw to finish the pattern:

3. G, 9

Page 250

1. Bug in pattern is shown:

2.

3. Bug in pattern is shown: K

Page 251

Answers will vary.

Page 252

1. surprised
2. mad
3. sad
4. silly

Science

Page 255

1. Vibration is quick movement back and forth.
2. You can feel the air vibrating.
3. They are waves that move through the air and into your ear.
4. It vibrates and passes sound vibrations to the inner ear.

Page 257

Answers will vary.

Page 258

window, yes
apple, no
rubber duck, no
glass of water, yes
book, no

Page 260

Circled words and phrases are shown for numbers 1–2:

1. thunder, a police siren
2. a flashlight, a whistle
3. Answers will vary.

Page 261

Likely groups are shown. Explanations will vary.

Group 1: flower, plant, tree, grass
Group 2: bread, carrot, apple, hot dog
Group 3: juice, milk, lake, rain

Page 262

Answers will vary.

Page 263

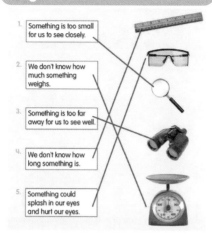

1. Something is too small for us to see closely.
2. We don't know how much something weighs.
3. Something is too far away for us to see well.
4. We don't know how long something is.
5. Something could splash in our eyes and hurt our eyes.

Page 265

1. hot or cold the air is
2. tool
3.–5. Answers will vary.

Page 267

1. ocean scientist
2. plant scientist, dinosaur scientist
3. rock scientist
4. Answers will vary.

Page 269

1. animals
2. give medicine to a horse
3.–5. Answers will vary.

Page 270

2.–3. Answers will vary.

Page 271

Likely groups are shown. Explanations will vary.

Group 1: duck, owl, eagle, bird

Group 2: sea horse, fish, whale, dolphin

Group 3: bear, cat, lion, dog

Page 272

Explanations will vary for items below:

1. a cat
2. an elephant
3. a bird

Page 273

Answers will vary.

Page 274

Answers will vary.

Page 275

Answers will vary.

Page 276

1. We put bug spray on ourselves because the smell keeps bugs off us.
2. We use nets to scoop up fish from the ocean.

Page 277

1. A hard bike helmet protects our heads.
2. We use bait to catch fish to eat.

Page 278

1. hunts
2. cries
3. sleeps
4. eats
5. drinks

Page 279

Answers will vary.

Page 281

1. Answers will vary.
2. summer; Explanations will vary.
3. The sun's light makes the moon shine.

Page 282

Answers will vary.

STEM

Page 287

Answers will vary.

Page 289

Answers will vary.

Page 293

Answers will vary.

Page 295

Answers will vary.

Page 296

Answers will vary.

Page 297

Answers will vary.

Page 298

Answers will vary.

Social Studies

Page 300

1. Clara's mom is at the bakery.

Page 301

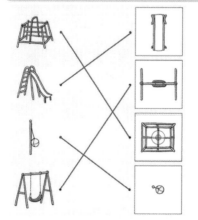

Page 302

Answers will vary.

Page 303

Answers will vary.

Page 305

1.–3. Answers will vary.

4. helps everyone say what they want

5. Answers will vary.

Page 306

Answers will vary.

Page 307

Answers will vary.

Page 308

Answers will vary.

Page 309

Answers will vary.

Page 311

1. Ⓐ

2. Ⓒ

3. Ⓐ

4.–5. Answers will vary.

Page 312

1. This is a pretty frame. <u>It was made in 1899.</u> <u>It is made of wood.</u>

2. This rocking horse <u>was made in 1920.</u> It is a beautiful horse. <u>Only 20 of them were made.</u>

3. Drawings will vary.

Page 313

Answers will vary.

Page 314

1. **Order** the photos from **first** to **last** to show how traveling has changed. Draw a line from the year to its picture.

2. Answers will vary.

Page 315

Answers will vary.

Page 317

1. went through lots of changes over time

2. made something work better

3. change

Page 318

Australia   India

Thailand   Tanzania

Page 319

Answers will vary.

Page 321

1. powders

2. smart

3. People throw colorful powders and spray colorful water.

4. They light bonfires, dance, and sing.

Page 322

Answers will vary.

Page 323

Page 328

Answers will vary.

Page 329

You say something mean.

You do something nice for someone.

You help someone.

You do not answer when someone talks to you.

You say something nice.

You yell at someone.

Page 330

Answers will vary.

Page 331

Answers will vary.

Page 332

Should Do:

1. wait for someone else to finish talking before you talk

2. think about other people's feelings

3. think about why you feel mad

Should Not Do:

4. scream when you feel mad

5. talk loudly when someone else is already talking

6. throw something when you feel mad

Page 333

Answers will vary.

Page 334

Answers will vary.

Page 335

Answers will vary.